CHEER UP
LOVE

Adventures in depression with the
CRAB of HATE

CHEER UP
LOVE

Adventures in depression with the
CRAB of HATE

SUSAN CALMAN

TWO
ROADS

www.tworoadsbooks.com

First published in Great Britain in 2016 by Two Roads
An imprint of John Murray Press
An Hachette UK company

1

A CIP catalogue record for this title is available from the British Library

Hardback ISBN 978 1 473 63200 4
Trade Paperback ISBN 978 1 473 63202 8
Ebook ISBN 978 1 473 63203 5
Audio Digital Download ISBN 978 1 473 63565 4

Typeset in Sabon MT by Palimpsest Book Production Ltd, Falkirk, Stirlingshire

Printed and bound in Great Britain by Clays Ltd, St Ives plc

Hodder & Stoughton policy is to use papers that are natural,
renewable and recyclable products and made from wood grown in
sustainable forests. The logging and manufacturing processes are expected
to conform to the environmental regulations of the country of origin.

Hodder & Stoughton Ltd
Carmelite House
50 Victoria Embankment
London EC4Y 0DZ

www.hodder.co.uk

For everyone who has been Cagney to my Lacey.

And to the Crab of Hate.

Without you I'm nothing.

CONTENTS

A SCENE FROM THE PRESENT DAY:
Morning has broken   1

INTRODUCTION:
Why I wrote this   5

DISCLAIMER:
I have no insurance anymore   11

CHAPTER 1
The Early Years: Growing up Susan   19

CHAPTER 2
The Crab of Hate: Understanding depression   29

CHAPTER 3
Cheer Up Love: What and what not to say   41

CHAPTER 4
You Are Not Alone: Depressives without borders   53

CHAPTER 5
I'm Not Mad Because I'm Gay:
Coming out and marriage   65

CHAPTER 6
To University and Beyond: Starring Amy Schumer   91

CHAPTER 7
Funny Crazy Lady: Mind your language   103

CHAPTER 8
So, What's It Like, Then? The day-to-day   115

CHAPTER 9
Tell Me How You're Feeling:
Talking, talking talking, happy talk   129

CHAPTER 10
I Can't Go to A Shrink, I'm Small Enough Already!
Shrink shopping   139

CHAPTER 11
The Tears of a Clown: Saved by stand-up   151

CHAPTER 12
Modern Life Is Awful: Twitter fun   165

CHAPTER 13
The Way We Look Tonight: Dressing for success   177

CHAPTER 14
Maybe It Is Your Fault: Whodunit   197

CHAPTER 15
Relationships: Dating   207

CHAPTER 16
Negativity Is My Superpower: A positive view   221

CHAPTER 17
So, What Are You Going to DO About It, Then?   233

CHAPTER 18
Some Nearly Final Thoughts   251

A SCENE FROM THE PRESENT DAY:
And in the end   255

ACKNOWLEDGEMENTS   257

USEFUL STUFF   259

ABOUT THE AUTHOR   261

A SCENE FROM THE PRESENT DAY: MORNING HAS BROKEN

DAWN breaks over Glasgow, as it always does, to the sound of snoring. My cats and wife combine in glorious harmony, voices reverberating and growling a tune that shakes my flat to the rafters. I try to extricate myself from the pile of fur and human but it's not easy. Cats, in particular, sleep with such sincerity that it seems a shame to wake them from their dreams, and there's an awkward scientific phenomenon that turns a tiny feline into the breathing equivalent of a boulder requiring the force of a bulldozer to shift them. In the end I'm forced to crawl out of the bottom of the bed, and after the pain of my contortion subsides, I take the time to congratulate myself for winning what is essentially a game of mammal Kerplunk.

I don't mind the fact that I'm left to my own devices for a while, in truth I enjoy a few solitary hours in the morning to appreciate the finer things in life. My first sip of strong coffee, the radio quietly playing in the background and the occasional After Eight for breakfast. It's at these times that I can truly appreciate what I have. Not in a material sense, of course. I don't have a huge house or a fancy car, and I'm certainly not dripping in diamonds, but that's never been my aim. At some points in my life I've been so miserable that I would have settled for being 'vaguely content' but I'm pleased to say that I've surpassed that lowly aim. Right now I can sincerely say that I am happy.

What's caused this shift of emotional tectonic plates? Well I've been with my wife for Fourteen years, married for four. I've several children (who are cats), a job I love, friends who support me and make me laugh, and a family who continue to put up with me despite the fact I embarrass them on a regular basis. Crucially, though, it's not just the people around me who make me happy. For the first time in my life one of the main sources of happiness is much closer to home. It's little old me. After decades of hating myself I've finally decided that maybe I'm not as bad as I first thought, that perhaps I have something of value to contribute to society. Not in a world-changing Mother Teresa way, but on a smaller, less religious scale. In the past couple of years I've even been known to throw myself a couple of compliments, a shocking turn of events which I couldn't have predicted if I was Derek Acorah.

In a bold move, I've finally embraced my idiosyncratic ways, accepted my eccentricities and wrapped my maudlin personality up in a bow to present to the world. I am what I am and I'm not sorry about that, unless I get drunk and insult someone. Which doesn't happen very often anymore. Sitting at my desk, writing this book, I'm well aware of the fact that my life could have gone in a very different direction. Through luck, hard work and persistence, I'm here and ready to tell my tale to the world.

And so this is it. I hope you enjoy it. I'm quite forceful in my opinions at times and I make no apology for that. Sadly, I can't make you like me. I'm not a hormone.

INTRODUCTION

HELLO. Welcome to this book. If you've bought it because you know who I am, welcome. If you've bought it because you liked the title, you have excellent taste. If you've been given it as a present, then please immediately thank whoever gave it to you because **they** have excellent taste. If you have no idea why you're reading this, then you're an impulse buyer and you should embrace that side of your personality. I too have bought things on whim. It's why I'm writing this while wearing a fully functioning Batman costume.

Just in case you've purchased this because of mistaken identity, let me start by introducing myself properly. My name is Susan Calman and at the time of writing this book I'm forty-one years old. I provide my age to you so you can place me in terms of your own history. If you're a youngster you might think I'm far too old to understand young people things. Let me assure you that you're wrong. I'm absolutely down with youth activities like table tennis and gin. If you're older than me then please be assured that I know a lot of people older than me and we get on fine. In fact, some would say that I am an old soul in a young body. I like darts, snooker and pubs with no music so you can have a decent conversation. I may in fact be a sixty-year-old man from Yorkshire.

It says 'writer' on my passport, mainly because I figured 'comedian' would cause problems when trying to gain entry to America. Saying that your job is a comedian is fraught with danger, especially when dealing with taxi drivers. The encounter usually goes one of two ways; either they ask you to tell them a joke, in which case my whimsical feminist view on life fails to raise a laugh. Or *they* tell you a joke, which can end badly for everyone. Before you get the wrong idea about me let me be clear: I love taxi drivers, I really do. Especially when they utter my favourite passive aggressive insult:

'Do you know who *is* funny? Kevin Bridges/Frankie Boyle/
Billy Connolly . . .' (repeats to fade)

I'm a writer, as this book illustrates, but I suppose I'm probably better known as a comedian. If you're a Radio 4 fan you'll have heard me on a multitude of shows like *The News Quiz* or *I'm Sorry I Haven't a Clue*. If you've only heard me on the wireless and don't know what I look like then let me assist. Imagine Angelina Jolie stuffed into the body of Kylie Minogue with a Scottish accent. If you've seen me on television, in shows like *Have I Got News For You* or *QI*, you'll know that I just lied a bit.

I'll talk about my height more as this book progresses, but suffice to say I'm short. I'm so short I can't see over counters, reach the card payment machines in petrol stations and if I buy three-quarter-length trousers they're still too long for my tiny little legs.

I am Scottish, from Glasgow to be precise. And I'd be very grateful if you could put aside any preconceptions you might of my hometown while you're reading this book. The media are often delighted to present my fellow Glaswegians as violent, drunken, drug-addicted louts filled with a dislike for the English. None of those tropes apply to me, and I'd hate you to think that any of the stories contained in these pages are a result of my innate Scottishness. It doesn't help my happiness quota living in a country where summer lasts for a week, but it's not the sole cause of my bleak outlook on life.

But let's get to the point of why we're all here. Me. And as we commence this thrill ride together, I think it's appropriate that I come out. Not about that! If you haven't worked out by the fact I'm wearing a Batman outfit that I'm a lady gay then I can't help you. And don't worry, much like the short issue you'll hear more stories of the fact I'm a very good friend of Dorothy later on. Those are the kind of juicy anecdotes that will get this book discussed in the comments section of the *Daily Mail*.

The coming out that I'm referring to is actually more difficult for me to admit than the fact that I'm gay. Because the truth is that I have depression.

In the past I've been diagnosed as having clinical depression but the medical diagnosis was, in a way, unnecessary.

Some things, like a broken leg, are very obvious. You see I'm not just a bit down sometimes, I'm depressed. I'm not like one of those little sad rabbits you sometimes see on a Hallmark card, I'm like a really upset Wookie. Full on, world-hating, can't stand anything or anyone – depression. For example, if I was to ask myself the standard happiness question – 'is this glass half full or half empty?' I'd say, 'there is no glass, I don't deserve a glass, I'll drink out of this cup of broken dreams while looking at photos on Facebook of people I went to school with who have a better glass than me.'

I was once so depressed that I'd thought *Bambi* was a comedy. I've known myself to be so down that when I eventually smiled I pulled a muscle in my eye. My depression was once so all-consuming that I couldn't even be bothered with personal grooming, like crimping my toe hair, and usually I like to make an effort when I wear sandals.

But I'm not alone, of course. Statistics from the Mental Health Foundation put my case into context: one in four people will experience some kind of mental health problem in the course of a year. Mixed anxiety and depression is the most common mental disorder in Britain, and women are more likely to have been treated for a mental health problem than men. It's something that affects more people in the United Kingdom that many would like to admit. I've decided to come clean about my mental health because, to be honest, people still seem rather embarrassed to talk about it. I've made no secret of how I feel, I've performed stand-up shows about my depression and indeed wrote an episode of my Radio 4 series *Susan Calman Is Convicted* about it.

I've become something of a poster girl for mental health now, which is a bit unexpected. I'd always hoped to become a poster girl of some sort but thought it might have been for my amazing muscles or my lovely hair. *'That's that mental comedian'* people say, which is fine. It's just another label, and society loves them. A journalist once asked me *'Is it difficult being a female Scottish lesbian comedian?'* I suggested it would be more difficult being a male Scottish lesbian comedian. They've never asked me for an interview again.

So many people got in touch with me after my show was broadcast on Radio 4, a couple of years ago, that I thought I'd write more about the subject. Partly because this is far cheaper than therapy, and partly because I truly believe that until more people start being honest about how they feel we will never get any better. And by 'we' I mean all of us. Those who have depression, those who live with us, work with us, care for us and even those who don't even believe that such a condition could exist.

The problem is that depression is like all-male comedy panel shows. No matter how much you want them to piss off, they're still there for everyone to see. It's a condition that doesn't necessarily disappear, but through the decades I've lived with it, I've developed coping mechanisms and strategies that mean I'm quite happy being unhappy. And I've written them all down for you.

Please be reassured as you read this, though, that I am absolutely fine now. You mustn't think that I wrote this while rocking back and forward in a darkened room covered in my own filth. I'm actually in an excellent place at the moment and have no doubt that I will continue to remain there. In fact, I'm so happy that I managed to write this book and I certainly couldn't have done that in the past, raking over my fetid memories and opening my heart to thousands of strangers. I am well, I am in a good place and I haven't been forced to write this as some form of community service or court ordered treatment.

They say that everyone has a book inside them and this is mine. Although I hope you buy the follow-up autobiography 'I cheered right up when I got the part of *Doctor Who*'. That's bound to happen in the next year or so. Fingers crossed.

DISCLAIMER:
I HAVE NO INSURANCE ANYMORE

IT may come as a surprise to some of you, but I wasn't always a clown. In fact, I used to have a proper job that required years of preparation. I went to university for four years, completed a diploma, trained for two years and then was a corporate lawyer for seven years. Yes, that's right. A highly paid corporate lawyer with a suit and a briefcase and money and a pension and sick leave and a future, until I gave it all up one day to be a stand-up comedian. I may have left my day job behind but, much like herpes, there's no real cure for being a lawyer. My previous employment seeps into almost all aspects of my life, not least the writing of this book. I don't mean that I've written it in Latin, although *cur non*? No. Instead, what I've been left with is a compulsion to set out a series of caveats to this book in order to be sure that there is no risk involved in what you're about to read. While there are a number of these disclaimers, the most important is undoubtedly this one:

DON'T DO WHAT I SAY OR DO.
I HAVE NO INSURANCE ANYMORE

I will tell you, in full and frank detail, some of the things that have happened to me in my life. I am not, in any way, recommending you do the same as me whether by way of treatment, relationships or life choices. In my view, comedians are not people that should be listened to without deep consideration being given to what we say. I often marvel at the way that some in the media rabidly seek out the political or sociological opinions of people who should have custard pies shoved in their faces. It's even more remarkable when people listen to us. I have never been persuaded to vote for a political party because someone I once saw doing ten minutes on *Live at the Apollo* told me to. I know that this sounds like I'm telling you to ignore the beautiful book you've just bought, and in a way I am. Because I've made some really, really stupid choices in my life, and through luck or fate some of them have worked out. Some of them definitely have not.

For example, I started doing stand-up comedy in my early thirties and was an open spot (the technical term for someone just starting out) for six months. Just six months during which I did five to ten minute sets in pubs and basements around the country. The most I earned was £10 for my time, certainly not enough to make me think that it would be a financially viable career. After what is considered a very short apprenticeship in comedy, I made the decision that I wanted to do the job full time.

In my head I've always been dynamic, and in the abstract have implemented a lot of bold decisions, but I've rarely acted on them because I am, in reality, an incredibly risk-averse person. But for some reason, on this occasion, I acted on my urges and went for it. That fateful day I walked into my boss's office, slammed a letter of resignation on his desk and flounced out declaring to anyone who would listen that I was going to be a star dammit! I'd love to say that what happened next was like a fairy tale, that I ended up walking straight into a TV job and moved to a mansion in London with my own bowling alley. The truth is that in my first year as a stand-up I earned £250. In my second year £400 and in my third year I think we got to the heights of £1,000.

You may well be reading this thinking, *That sounds amazing Susan, I'll do the same.* Please don't, not unless you are totally sure. Don't get me wrong, changing my job was absolutely the best thing that I could have done for my mental health. I loved being a lawyer but found the restrictive atmosphere of the Scottish legal community, with its occasional misogyny and slight homophobia, utterly horrific and couldn't wait to get out.

I didn't feel resigning was such a big deal because I always felt I could go back to the law. Although I suspect accusing them of homophobia and misogyny might now rule that out. Of course, it was brilliant to take charge of my destiny in that way. It was like a scene from a film where the lead character runs away to chase a ridiculous dream. But, please, I don't want to be responsible for a rash of resignations all over the country as people 'do a Calman'.

I'm slightly disparaging about my old profession but the truth is I loved the job and I'm still a lawyer at heart. I used to specialise in the Data Protection Act (the sexiest of all statutes), and my past life means I'm one of the only people in the world who looks forward to being cold-called so I can have an opportunity to chat about the use of personal information. I know. I'm very popular at parties. My past as a solicitor leaches into almost every part of my life. For example, when I'm performing on stage I tend to think of the gig as a negotiation. I put forward my position, the audience agree or disagree, and eventually we come to a conclusion which may, or may not, be to my benefit.

As a recovering solicitor I want to give you the contractual small print right up front. It's not that I'm trying to wriggle out of any responsibility for what I've written; rather I want the terms of the contract between you (hereinafter known as The Reader) and myself (hereinafter known as The Writer). Please read this section and nod at the end to show your agreement. I won't know if you've actually nodded. I need to take that on trust.

The Writer would like The Reader to be aware that:

1. Despite the fact I've watched an awful lot of *Casualty* on the BBC, I am not a qualified doctor. I therefore cannot give medical advice. If you have any concerns of the health nature go and see your GP. If your GP doesn't listen keep going until you find someone who listens to you. Someone will listen to you.

2. I have not consulted the medical profession regarding the contents of this book as it's a personal memoir of my own experiences. I'd love to write a proper academic textbook on the subject, but thought it better that I write about what I know, namely me. The only academic book I could write with any intellectual gravitas would be '101 ways to use macaroni cheese in everyday life'.

3. I have particular views on therapy and medication which are very much my own. Depression is a curious thing, as each person is affected in a very different way by it. You need to find your own way to make it work for you.

4. I am definitely a woman, but this is not just a book for ladies. Depression is something that affects old and young, men and women. In fact, sometimes I think men find talking about their depression slightly more difficult because of historic gender preconceptions. I've tried to make this book applicable to everyone, but I am a girl, so if I have made any sweeping generalisations based on my genetic make-up I apologise in advance. You can find me in the playground, pull my hair and run away.

5. You may find some of the content self-indulgent. I make no apologies for that. This is clearly labelled as a book about depression. If you thought you were buying a Rom Com or a book about One Direction then I honestly worry for you. Although, in the interests of full disclosure, I love One Direction. And I'm not ashamed to say it.

6. I may retell 'back in the day stories'. By that I mean tales of times gone past when people used to walk to school in bare feet. I say that because technology and access to information has changed the way that people feel about and deal with depression. I sometimes wish I were younger now as I wouldn't feel as isolated as I did when I was growing up. Then I look at Twitter and thank goodness I grew up when I did. I couldn't have coped with the grammar pedantry, never mind my own self-hatred.

7. I use a lot of metaphors and similes in this tome. I may also contradict myself at times. Don't get upset about it. It shows that this was written by an actual human being and not some robot programmed to only ever make sense. Of course, if you want a book that makes complete sense and has no mistakes I'd recommend you never read anything ever again and instead simply watch some television. Maybe *Antiques Roadshow*. That always calms me down.

8. Don't be offended if I seem light-hearted regarding some of the topics in this book. It's how I deal with things. If you are easily offended you should probably stop reading now. But then you probably stopped reading when I mentioned I was Scottish.

9. I relate a number of very honest stories because I hope they might help you or you might find them interesting. Some of them are very personal and extremely uncomfortable for me to disclose. In fact, the process of writing this book has been more difficult than I thought it would be. I don't think I quite understood how emotional it would be writing down some of these anecdotes and retelling some of the worst moments from my life. All I ask is that if, after reading this book, if you meet me or come and see me at a gig, don't look at me any differently. Admitting you have depression doesn't make you weak, and you most certainly shouldn't pity me. I'm exactly the same person you've been listening to or watching for the past few years. Feel free to ask me any questions you have, but please don't let it affect our relationship. We're still going to SnapChat each other, right?

All clear? Lovely. Then let us begin.

CHAPTER 1

THE EARLY YEARS: GROWING UP SUSAN

AS we start to delve into my tale of sadness, I think it's important that I explain my family situation and upbringing to help you understand why I've ended up the way I am. If you're a comic book fan it's sort of my depression origin story. And to non-nerds reading this, I mean it's the way I got my superpowers of sadness. A radioactive spider bit Spiderman, Wolverine was a mutant who was then experimented on, and I collected thimbles when I was younger. Of course, I'm lucky in that I don't even need to wear a cape to invoke my superpowers. And I certainly wouldn't change in a phone booth either. Have you been in one recently? The smell is enough to burn your nose hair off. The only time I've ever genuinely wondered if I could develop a superpower was when I was bitten on the left breast by a guinea pig (it's a long story). I sat in the dark for hours waiting for my special abilities to appear, Susan Calman Guinea Pig Woman! I have no idea what would happen if I became such a hybrid hero. I understand that these furry rodents eat their own faeces, so that was something to look forward to.

Some of us may have realised we were maudlin at an early age; many others happily float through life until something triggers their depression far later on. I like to think I'm textbook. Depressed as a child, teenager and adult. Don't be jealous now, I'm just one of life's winners.

I was born in 1974 in Glasgow, the youngest of three children. My mum was a primary school teacher, my dad was a doctor and we lived in a house with our two dogs in an unremarkable area of the city. Sadly for the tabloid press, I have no tales of childhood cruelty to reveal, and I'm absolutely aware of the fact that I lived a comfortable and privileged life. There is no empirical evidence to show that the way I was brought up is in any way to blame for the way I feel now.

But, of course, despite the normality of my early years, I entirely blame my parents for everything. What kind of stand-up comedian/depressive would I be if I didn't firmly lay responsibility at the people who have done the most to look after me? The holy grail of sadness is trying to find the root cause of why we are the way that we are, and the easiest option is to look right at your own doorstep. My own theories are wrong, of course, my upbringing isn't the sole reason for the way that I am; however, there are possibly some environmental conditions that mean I didn't deal with my feelings in a healthy way until far later on in my life.

I was always of the impression while growing up that

excess emotion was something to be avoided. Being a 'hysterical woman' was the most awful of all criticisms because it's quite pejorative. Talking about feelings didn't seem to be encouraged, because who knows where that kind of talk would lead. More than anything I wanted to be a plucky woman like Doris Day who, despite all that life threw at her, maintained a sunny disposition throughout. But I couldn't. A dark cloud followed me around all the time. I was like Eeyore the donkey, but less optimistic. And I didn't tell anyone how bad it was, initially because it didn't seem appropriate, but as time went on the fear of expressing emotions was almost as bad as the emotions themselves.

As I've got older, the thing I've realised helps me control my depression the most is talking about how I feel, but it's a very new thing for me to embrace. Talking to children about their emotions wasn't really de rigueur in the 70s and 80s; let's face it, educational establishments were still caning children for breaking rules. I often marvel when I see children out with their parents in the present day and hear how some families, at least, communicate. I was in a coffee shop the other day trying to write this very book. I'd read somewhere that taking yourself out of your normal working environment could spark new ideas. After four hours I'd had so much coffee that my only creative idea was making a chart to measure how often I needed to go to the toilet. After my fifth visit in an hour, my attention was drawn to a young mother and her small son at an adjacent table. The boy was sitting rather glumly, ignoring all proffered toys and snacks. In my youth I would probably have been left to get on with it. Not in this day and age.

> Mother: You seem a little sad Charlie. Are you feeling OK?
>
> Charlie: I'm just sad.
>
> Mother: Let's talk about it then.

What? Talk about it! With your mother! Are we living in some sort of hippy commune now? Communicating your feelings when politely asked to do so? Witchcraft I tell you! Witchcraft! Even now, as a born again chatter, I still have a physical reaction when I try to talk about what's inside my head. Like there's a blockage in my pipes preventing me from letting it all out. My vocabulary reduces and I've found myself expressing feelings through a series of grunts and snorts, so unnatural is the idea of saying the things that are in my head out loud.

I'll be honest, though, it's not all my parents' fault. I'll concede that I was a strange child. When I was in Primary Six my school put on a performance of *Casey Jones*. I was chosen to play the plum part of Mrs Jones. Of course I was, I was always a drama queen. I enjoyed the prospect of being the female lead but had some problems with the script. My teacher insisted that I hadn't put enough inflection into the emotional lyrics where the widow in question seemed almost cheerful about the prospect of meeting a new husband somewhere up the railway line. I resisted the director's interpretation at the time, despite being only ten, as I didn't think Mrs Jones would move on that quickly after the demise of her husband.

When you constantly see the negatives in life it's difficult. The question 'what's the worst that could happen' was more of a mantra for me. And growing up I could see the worst-case scenario in everything. A trip to the shops, a game of Snap, even choosing what to wear was fraught with emotion. At the age of nine I was late to a school trip to the pantomime because I refused to put on a pair of corduroy dungarees that had elastic around the ankles. In my head I was worried that if something slipped down the top of the dungarees it would get stuck in the leg, and this would keep happening and happening and happening until eventually I would be so weighed down by my own dungarees that I wouldn't be able to walk. At the time it seemed totally reasonable. But the point is that you weren't meant to talk about these things. I couldn't possibly explain to my mother that I was frightened of being incapacitated by jelly babies without her questioning my grasp on reality.

As I grew older my outlook on life got even worse. Why? Well, for starters I became a teenager. Being a hormonal and confused teen is bad enough at the best of times, but if you start off from a position of general dislike of the world it's even worse. I was running the hundred metres of despair with a ninety-nine-metre head start. But, like a true Brit, I kept quiet.

I believe it's a general truth that, certainly when I was younger, we weren't encouraged to be emotionally expressive. Of course that's changing, although not necessarily in a good way. The needle has swung quite dramatically in the other direction leading to a certain cynicism about the truth of emotional declarations. I lay the blame squarely at the raft of Saturday night entertainment shows where young people lay their entire lives out for millions to hear, all in the hope of getting fifteen minutes of fame in a talent show. Television producers quickly realised that it was gold for an audience of repressed Brits to watch the slow unravelling of a teenager while they were singing a tuneless rendition of Mariah Carey or Whitney Houston.

'It's my last chance!' wails a sixteen-year-old child as the forty-one-year-old me sits in my pants wondering whether or not their pain is sufficient for me to text a number. 'I'm doing it for me Nan!' as Twitter goes into overdrive debating whether or not the tears that are being produced are enough to allow us, the great British public, to grant them another week of public torture. Of course, I would never infer that the veracity of the stories is questionable, but I don't even flinch when I see a contestant have a breakdown on a Saturday night. And those who have no issues are labelled boring. In truth, anything is more palatable when dressed up in flashing lights with the input of a stylist and the editing of a producer. I'd love to enter *The X Factor*, stand on stage and say:

'I'm doing this because I feel empty all the time. I have nothing and no one. My life is worth nothing.' (Pause) 'I'm going to sing "If I Said You Had A Beautiful Body Would You Hold It Against Me". Thanks.'

I'm not suggesting that you should pour your heart out at the drop of a hat. No. It's not always good to express yourself emotionally to just anyone, and it's crucial to get to the point where you want to talk in your own time. I appreciate the irony of my writing about how important it is to talk, then in the next paragraph telling you you shouldn't, but your thoughts are precious and shouldn't be revealed willy-nilly. In my experience, unless experiences are honestly expressed to the right person it's like throwing biscuits into a tumble dryer.

The truth is that I was definitely depressed from a very early age, but to be fair none of us realised what I had. Without question the understanding of children's mental health has increased greatly in the intervening years and, if I was at school now, the fact that I was having difficulties would have been picked up and dealt with sooner. Whether or not I would have admitted it is a different matter, because as a child, far more frightening to me than expressing my emotions, were the consequences of expressing them. I was absolutely terrified of being labelled as 'mad'. I'd watched *Suddenly, Last Summer*; I'd heard tales of Gartnavel Royal, the imposing psychiatric hospital in Glasgow that looked like a prison set back from the 'normal' hospital where 'normal people' were treated. I was pretty sure that if I told anyone how I felt I'd end up in a straitjacket and that my future would be ruined. Who would want to employ a nutter? Who would want to marry a mental person? My tactics for survival were simple, keep my mouth shut, keep a smile on my face and don't tell anyone how I was feeling.

Which was the worst possible thing I could have done, because by not talking I ended up in a quite terrible place. I felt alone, isolated, confused about why I just couldn't make myself happy. I should have been, I knew I should have been, I just couldn't make it happen. It's the same feeling of frustration I get now when I come home from Ikea with a flat-pack bookcase that, after hours of work, I put together and seem to have made a bed. I'd started cutting myself, a common thing to do among many depressives, and I still have scars on my arms from that time. I hate them. I see them every day as a reminder of how I felt, of the frustration and anger that was directed towards myself. I would sit in my room punishing myself for my own mind, and being singularly unable to know what to do about it.

Unsurprisingly, after years of keeping quiet, everything fell apart in a rather horrific way. I tried to kill myself. I took a load of pills one day because I just couldn't see any way out. And of all of the things that I admit in this book, this is unquestionably the most difficult for me. I've tried to talk about it on stage and in a previous stand-up show I mentioned it, only to find audiences reacting in very different ways. Some people were shocked, some laughed because it made them feel nervous. My favourite moment was when I was in the middle of a show in Glasgow. I stood centre stage and said, 'I tried to kill myself.' There was silence in the room until one man leaned forward and quietly asked:

'Did you manage it?'

Yes, yes I did. I am the ghost of myself come back to haunt you all. I love Glasgow.

I'll skip over some of the details involved in this part of my story because it's actually still surprisingly difficult to write. And it's also nice to keep some air of mystery around me. Suffice to say that at the age of sixteen everything had become so awful in my head that I ended up being sectioned and sent to an adolescent psychiatric ward in that scary hospital in Glasgow. I hope you like the way I said that really quickly like it was no big deal. Except it was a big deal.

I'm not going to sugar-coat this for you, it was awful. I'd love to be able to tell you that I felt supported and loved and cared for. But I didn't. I was terrified. No doors on the toilets or the showers, being watched twenty-four hours a day. There were some incredibly disturbed people in the hospital with me, who were clearly frightened of themselves and the staff. All I could think about was that they could keep me in there as long as they wanted, that I'd lost control of my life and my freedom. The upshot was that when I met with the doctors, I would have said anything to get out of there. Anything. And I did. I said what they wanted me to say and was released after a few days. I said that I was fine, and I was sorry for frightening everyone and it was just a hormonal blip and that I would never ever scare people again. I was normal, and cured and happy. Of course I wasn't.

It did 'help' me in one way. I resolved to never, ever, tell anyone how I felt again. Because I could never, and would never, go back to that kind of place again. And so my teenage years ended with my mouth clamped shut, my depression hidden firmly inside and a knowledge that if I didn't pretend to be OK, I could end up back in that nightmare.

I didn't tell the truth about the contents of my head for years. Which, as you can imagine, wasn't a good move. But on the grand scale of things it seemed better to be depressed than terrified. And that's how I stayed. Sad and terrified, but at least I was free.

CHAPTER 2

THE CRAB OF HATE

UNDERSTANDING DEPRESSION

I'D like to get a handle on what depression is, but let's face it, it's not particularly easy to explain. The condition isn't a definite thing that you can stick a badge on and say 'that's depression'. You can't point to it in an identity parade, because it's not just one thing; it changes, it varies, it leaves and it comes back in a different form, but remains resolutely the same. Depression reminds me of a character in a soap opera that inexplicably returns to the show despite dying in a horrible accident the year before, and being played by a different actor. And no one ever mentions it.

Sometimes I wish that just before my down times occur, a physical symptom would appear, like a rash or something, which would be an early warning sign of an impending attack. At least then I would know to prepare myself. Sadly, it's a stealthy bugger with more characters than an episode of *Game of Thrones*. Sometimes before I become depressed I lose my appetite. Sometimes I want to eat all the food in the world. Sometimes I can't sleep.

Sometimes I sleep for hours. Of course, all of the symptoms listed are also indicative of other conditions or, more commonly, just things that happen seasonally. When autumn arrives I seem to have a subconscious requirement to hibernate, and so eat as much as possible to keep me going in the long winter months. There are times when I can be tired, not tired, hungry or full, and it's nothing to do with my state of mental health.

Depression is a tough thing to understand even for some medical experts, and even more difficult for some to comprehend because there's no one cause of it. It's not infectious, although I have been known to bring a party to a grinding halt. It can be frustrating when you can't just open a book and find an answer, although you can search for it on the Internet. Please be warned, though, the Internet contains a can of worms you might not want to open.

Some people have a perception that small things like the weather can make you depressed, as if the solution is to move somewhere where it's always sunny. Because Los Angeles is such a hotbed of mental stability, isn't it? It's never the weather that makes me depressed; the fact that it rains most of the year suits my temperament. If it were sunny it would be strange. Like seeing a Goth in a swimming costume. Scotland has a pretty bad record when it comes to sunshine but the whole population isn't down all the time, we just get to look forward to the fortnight of tepid sunshine we get that's spread over June, July and August.

I'm not depressed because of my nationality, although the attitude to my country can spark feelings of impotent rage. Often when I appear on a panel show someone will make a joke about heroin/deep fried Mars bars/the fact that I won't know what fruit or veg is. The image of the dour Scotsman isn't true; but I acknowledge that I do sometimes look rather annoyed at life. But that's usually after someone has just insulted my country. In fact, I'd like to take this opportunity to say something that's been on my mind for a while. If you are reading this and you write jokes for television, please stop saying we're all unhealthy. Of course people in Scotland drink, as do people in England. Last time I was in Newcastle I saw a man dressed as a jar of Colman's Mustard crying on the pavement. The only thing that consoled me was that somewhere else in Newcastle there was a man dressed as a joint of ham, equally drunk, trying to find his condiment friend. To say that Scots are ignorant, violent, drunken, drug addicted is an insulting generalisation. Like the generalisation that all the people who write jokes for television are lazy shits.

The best way to describe my standard state of mind when I'm depressed is that it's a bit like when your laptop goes onto power saving mode. Everything is just a little bit dim. And for as long as I can remember that's the way I've thought. The earliest indication that I was different from other children was when I described classic children's show *Bagpuss* as 'that show with the dead, stuffed cat'. As I said in a previous chapter, growing up in the 1970s and 80s, it was clear that no matter how bad things were it was not the done thing to talk about it.

There's a strange dichotomy in British society you see. We're never meant to look unhappy but if you start to talk about how you feel people run a mile. The perception of enjoyment is key. I remember my family used to holiday every summer on an island off the coast of Scotland. There are countless pictures of me and my brother and sister swimming in the sea. The same sea that oil workers are given survival suits for in case they fall in, because exposure to the freezing temperatures can kill you in minutes. But we swam in it with only a BHS swimming costume for protection. And I clearly recall, as I no longer felt my lower limbs and my lips turned blue, my mother holding a camera and shouting, 'Smile! It looks like you're not having fun!'

My depression can last for varying periods of time; sometimes I can snap out of it within minutes, at other times it takes far longer to get back on an even keel. In fact, I often measure my depression in terms of box sets rather than time, as it makes me feel slightly less bad about hiding myself away. So instead of saying 'I sat in the dark for a week' I say 'I stayed in bed for all seven series of *The West Wing*'. Another time it only lasted as long as the first three series of *Jonathan Creek*. That was a good spell. American shows are undoubtedly better for a depressive than UK ones, simply because they last longer. Even if you binge-watch every series of *The Thick of It,* it won't see you through a bad spell in the same way that eleven seasons of *Bones* will. Although Peter Capaldi swearing is far more cheerful than watching some attractive Americans dissect bodies.

Most annoyingly, depression can sometimes be triggered with absolutely no warning at all. The strangest and simplest of encounters can set me off in a spiral of discontent. Of course, the most common is a social media encounter. Out of nowhere and apropos of nothing I'll get a tweet that says 'you're not funny' or 'I prefer Sandi Toksvig' (who doesn't) or 'you're fat'. My wife always knows when I've had one of these encounters. When I'm particularly stressed I have a habit of flattening my fringe repeatedly. She says she can tell when I've had a bad day when she comes home and George Formby answers the door.

But many other less obvious things can set me off. Worrying about the future, worrying about the past. I'm cursed with an excellent memory and so can quite easily be sent into a spiral of despair remembering an episode that can be decades old. For example, I drove past a pub in the West End of Glasgow recently. I had driven along that road many times in the past twenty years but for some reason on this day I looked to my left and saw the frontage of an establishment that I'd spent many hours in while I was a student. Depression is a cruel beast that has the capacity to wipe all of the happy times that may have taken place and instead replaces them with one large black hole filled with a whole lot of awful. And so it happened this day, when instead of thinking of the friends I'd made and the trivia quizzes I'd enjoyed, my mind was filled with memories of an evening when an acquaintance had made a chance remark that has remained in my subconscious for twenty years. I remembered every detail. It was a rainy November night, possibly around my birthday, and I was meeting some university mates for a drink. I was single (a standard state of affairs in those days) and was determined to make an effort in order to get some sort of action. I'll talk more about my appearance later in the book, all you need to know right now is that my standard apparel involved cherry red Doc Martens, an old Canadian army coat I'd found in a second-hand shop, a baggy wool jumper and lots and lots of different coloured Levis. This particular night I'd mixed things up a bit and had borrowed my flatmate's tight T-shirt, short skirt and long boots. I suspect I'd seen *Pretty Woman* and decided that Julia Roberts was the right fashion role model for me. I arrived at the pub, feeling rather awkward out of my usual comfort zone of Morrissey crossed with K.D. Lang, but hoping that I'd have one of those Rom Com moments where I swept into the bar to applause from the general public astonished at the beauty that had been hidden for so long. I teetered in (the boots had heels) and rested my arm on the bar, tapped one of my mates on the shoulder and prepared for the adoration that would occur. My friend turned round, looked me up and down and said, very deliberately, 'What the fuck are you wearing Susan. You look like a pig in knickers.' I, metaphorically, crumpled to the ground and, literally, walked out of the pub, straight home, and back into my dungarees and heavy boots. I haven't tried to wear a skirt since that day. Now my friend (who unsurprisingly I haven't spoken to since we left university) probably won't even remember saying that to me and I'm sure had absolutely no idea the effect that her comments made. But I do. Depression is a mental scrapbook of hell playing straight into my brain every single day of the week.

Films can set me off. For example, I refuse to watch films about sad robots because they can send me into a pit of despair that can last for weeks. The reason for this is, of course, a childhood trauma. When I was a young-ster I watched two films in quick succession that had a long-lasting effect on me. The first was *Silent Running* starring Bruce Dern. The film ends (spoiler alert) with a drone tenderly caring for the last biological specimens of earth. The sight of the tiny robot watering flowers, knowing it was the last vestige of humanity, was too much for me. The idea that a robot would have a soul is, for some reason, the most utterly astonishing thing. I know, dear reader, you might be able to tell already, but one of the reasons for my depression is the fact I tend to over-think things. Subsequent to that I was plonked in front of the television to watch the Walt Disney classic *The Black Hole*, where another robot called B.O.B. was killed while being a hero. The utter devastation I felt while watching these films means that I will never watch *AI* or *WALL-E*. I have enough self-awareness to know that any hint of robot heroics will make we wail like I did when I was a kid.

Depression is often referred to as 'The Invisible Illness' because of the lack of immediate physical signs, which has both positive and negative consequences. On the posi-tive side, the fact that you wouldn't know that I was falling apart inside just by looking at me means that I can hide how I'm feeling and carry on with work and life without fear of prejudice or discrimination. Because, let's face it, admitting you have a mental health problem to some people, especially in a work environment, can change the way that some people perceive you. I can just imagine the HR meeting:

HR manager: Just to let you know that Susan Calman in Corporate is having a hard time just now.

HR minion: Is there anything we can do to help?

HR manager: Not really. She has (whispers) depression.

HR minion: Is it safe to let her carry on working?

HR manager: I think she's OK, but I have locked the cutlery drawer in the staff kitchen.

However, the lack of a plaster or a bandage can be negative for exactly the same reason. Just by looking at me you'll have no idea what's happening in my head. It's a condition that you have to positively admit to others, not something that can necessarily be worked out. When I had a proper job I was terrified of admitting to anyone that I had depression, because if I did it would go on my permanent file and, rightly or wrongly, that it might affect my career progression. It was bad enough that I was a woman who might disappear off to have children at some point. I have some sympathy with my employers though. A depressed, gay woman is a triple threat of potential employment discrimination cases.

The word 'depression' is itself inadequate in trying to

explain the condition. There are countless levels that can be experienced ranging from

'I'm a bit sad today.'
to
'I've been really down for a while now.'
to
'I don't think I can go on.'

Let's not be precious about this, though there are depression snobs among us. People who are pleased when they're demonstrably more miserable than others. I've had genuine conversations with friends when we've attempted to 'out miserable' each other. One of the least attractive aspects of being depressed is the fact that you live in a tunnel of darkness and you can't imagine that anyone could ever understand how you're feeling. I had a friend who I became incredibly frustrated at because she believed that she was suffering more than anyone ever had or indeed ever will. A fight between two angry, morose women is very uncomfortable to watch, never mind take part in.

But whatever the definition there's undoubtedly a difference between just being a bit down, which happens to all of us, and being properly depressed.

True depression isn't something you can just get over, like a twenty-four-hour cold or food poisoning. You can't just say, 'After I ate at that Thai place I had terrible depression, I'm not eating there again.' In fact, little annoys me more than when I'm standing, minding my own business, and someone approaches me with words: 'What's wrong with your face? Smile.' I want to grab them by the lapels and scream, 'Why? What if my whole family has been wiped out in a tragic accident, I've lost my job and I've woken up with a turnip instead of a face? I'm turnip woman! How will I find love if my face is like a turnip!'

It can be so difficult to characterise what we're feeling that it's common to try to articulate it by giving it a personality or a character of its own. My friend has given her depression a name, so that when she's feeling down she says, 'Bertha's come for a visit.' We all know a visit from Bertha is not a good thing, but it's easier to send a message suggesting an unwanted friend won't leave than try to explain what kind of sadness is hanging over her.

Many people compare their depression to an animal and one of the most common is, as Churchill expressed it, a black dog. Although he self-medicated in a way I wouldn't necessarily recommend:

> 'My rule of life prescribed as an absolutely sacred rite, smoking cigars and also the drinking of alcohol before, after and if need be during all meals and in the intervals between them.'

I have a similar animal-based description of my depression. One which sums up, in the best way possible, how I feel when I'm in the middle of my own personal episode of *Bleak House*. I call it my 'Crab of Hate', which I know sounds like a really ineffective Pokémon. Out of the blue, and without expecting it, the Crab of Hate climbs up my back, pinches both of my earlobes and whispers gently to me. He always whispers in English, by the way, not crab language. That would be difficult to understand. The Crab of Hate tells me all the things I don't want to hear, the things that make me doubt myself and hate myself.

'No one likes you. No one would miss you if you weren't here. Why do you even bother? Everyone laughs at you when you leave the room. You're useless. And you smell.'

It might sound a little silly or childlike to make up these kinds of characters but for me it makes the whole thing easier to explain. I told my wife about him (and it is a him) and now all I need to say to her is that 'the Crab is about' and she knows what I'm going through.

It helps me to visualise my enemy, so that I can picture what's happening to me. All I need to do is shake the Crab off and I'll be better. Sometimes all it takes is a shake of the head to be rid of him. Sometimes his grip is quite firm and I need the help of others to throw him back into the sea. He is my constant crustacean companion and he's as much a part of my life now as the rest of my family.

It can be quite positive to find a way of trying to give a personality to the way that you feel, if only so you can have a sliding scale for your own reference of how you're feeling. It can be helpful to use existing frames of reference. Perhaps

'I'm feeling a bit Kathy Bates in Misery.'
or
'I have a cloud following me round, I'm Perkin the Flump.'

Perkin the Flump was the first depressed character I ever encountered. Apart from Orville the Duck.

You might think it's a slightly foolish endeavour to create a character around your own particular feelings, but give it a go. It can help create shorthand for reference that, as with my wife, can make things easier to explain to people. Then your nearest and dearest can more easily understand what's going on.

The Crab of Hate is as much part of me as my genetic code, or my love of cats, or my hatred of warm weather. He's been sitting on my shoulders for my whole life. You can't see him in photographs, because he always scuttles away, but you can see the effect he has on me. We are connected. He is me and I am him. A double act contracted for a summer season at the end of the pier, and the season never ends. The trick is not to let him take the spotlight by himself.

CHAPTER 3

CHEER UP, LOVE: WHAT AND WHAT NOT TO SAY

WHY have I called this book *Cheer Up Love*? Because I'm hoping that if you're someone who doesn't wrestle with depression you might read this book and understand that it's one of the worst things you could possibly say to someone who's feeling down. Don't get me wrong; I'm acutely aware of how difficult it can be to communicate with someone who's disappeared down a well of despair, but cheerily shouting down at us while we're treading water, rather than throwing us a life belt, doesn't help. Depression is the only condition I've ever encountered where people think that being a bit patronising is a way of trying to cure an illness.

My wife broke her kneecap a few years ago. She says it was my fault. To be fair, on retelling the story, I can see where she's coming from. We had been on a night out and got some chips and curry sauce as a delicious treat. She was running up the stairs to our flat and I was chasing her to try and get the chips back. Because I'd paid for the chips so technically they were my property. In her haste she slipped and fell, but neither of us realised that she'd seriously injured herself and so we simply ate the chips (delicious!) and went to bed. It was only when I found her collapsed on the bathroom floor a few hours later that I had an inkling the situation was serious. I'll never forget the look on the doctor's face at A & E as she explained the cause of her injury was that she'd slipped in a stairwell when her wife was chasing her for chips. I'm sure he was thinking that it was like *Sex and the City* had come to life in front of his very eyes. The upshot was that she was in pain and on crutches for several weeks. Not once, in the time that she was recovering, did anyone tip their head gently to one side and in a quiet voice say, 'Why don't you just walk properly love?'

People who say 'cheer up love' to me have often regretted it because it makes me angry. Very angry. I have a terrible temper unfortunately, like a Tasmanian devil on speed, and while I try to keep it under control there are times when I lose it. I'm not proud of myself at getting so upset, but the people who cheerily suggest all I need to do is get over myself can have no idea of what I've gone through just to leave the house. Sometimes I wake up feeling completely lost with life. I've avoided the mirror because I think I look like the Hunchback of Notre Dame on a bad day. I've managed to drag myself out of the protective cocoon of my flat to go to the shops or the post office, tried to avoid crying as I'm buying milk. I've found myself wandering around the street wondering what the hell I'm doing with my life. And at those times, when I'm at my lowest ebb, the worst possible thing that can happen is be greeted by a cheery man loudly exclaiming, 'Cheer up love!'

'I COULD IF I WOULD MATE! IF I COULD STOP MY STUPID HEAD FROM MAKING ME MISERABLE I'D BE DELIGHTED! I DON'T WANT THIS! I DON'T LIKE THIS! I HATE EVERYTHING ABOUT MYSELF! DO YOU HEAR ME? I HATE MYSELF!'

I have, on numerous occasions, sat in front of a mirror trying to reason with myself, hoping against hope that simply through the force of my own mind I could cheer up. The logical part on my brain knows that those people are just trying to be nice, that they see a sad person who in their mind needs a little bit of cheeriness to help it all just go away. But it really doesn't help.

'Cheer up love' is at the very top of my list of comments that can actually make me feel more depressed than I did before. There are many others of course, including, but not limited to:

1. *'It could be worse!'* No. No it couldn't. Right at this moment, in my head, nothing could be worse. I couldn't feel more awful and ugly and sad. The only thing that could make me feel even more upset is someone pointing out that there is a possibility that life could be more horrific. I know you're trying to help, I know you're trying to be happy and in some way, by osmosis, make me feel better, but it really doesn't help. Right now is the worst it could be. Leave me to my misery

and this giant bowl of mashed potato I've made for myself.

2. 'At least you don't have a cactus/flower/potato growing out of your head/cancer.' I get this one. I really do. With so many people suffering in the world with incurable diseases and terrible inoperable conditions, it's true that being really sad isn't the worst thing that could happen. The problem is that being reminded of that fact can just make us feel worse. Because then we feel like our particular medical problem isn't worth bothering about because it's not as bad as what others are going through. But illness isn't a competition. It's not a game of top trumps of who has it worse. One of the reasons that people with mental health issues often become as ill as they do is the fear that what they have isn't a 'real' problem. That they don't want to take up the time of their GP. We don't have cancer, we don't have a cactus growing out of our heads, but we have a problem that should, and could, be helped. And the sooner it is addressed the better.

3. 'What have you got to be miserable about?' This is also pretty common, and it's partly because people with mental health issues are so bloody good at hiding it. MI5 should start recruiting depressed people as undercover operatives because we are, without question, the most qualified people in the world to live a double life. When Daniel Craig retires I'd like to see a James Bond who, after some light killing and sexual adventures, spends a whole weekend on his sofa eating the contents of his fridge and crying at a video of a three-legged dog someone put on Facebook.

The problem is there's a preconception that in order to be depressed you have to have something to be depressed about. 'Oh she lost her job and her house and her husband left her, I see why she's a bit down.' If you have a career and a nice flat and a partner who loves you, sometimes it's difficult for people to understand what the problem is. But again, pointing out what we already know is unhelpful. I can't tell you how many times I've noted the obvious to myself. I have a wife who loves me, I have somewhere nice to live, I have lovely friends, I have a wonderful family and I have a job that I love. I should be the happiest woman in the world. But I'm not. Pointing that out just makes me feel worse. That I'm selfish and ungrateful. Outward signs of success don't mean inner happiness. You never know what anyone is going through unless they tell you.

4. 'Oh just pull yourself together!' Sure. No problem. I wish I'd thought of that myself. I'll just do that right now. Apologies for bothering everyone, all I needed was for a total stranger to tell me to just get over it. Stiff upper lip. Thanks for your contribution.

5. 'What's wrong with you now?' A statement that is usually accompanied by an exasperated sigh, this is a particularly excellent one because it plays right into the paranoia part of my depression, the bit that the Crab of Hate excels at. By asking what the problem is *now*, it clearly indicates not only that people have noticed a problem in the past, but that it's also becoming annoying. It has an immediate and terrifying effect of making me think, *Everyone's pissed off at me for being miserable all the time aren't they! I should just keep it quiet and pretend I'm fine and then people won't avoid me in the street in case I moan!*

6. 'Smile! It might never happen!' I think it has. Because I'm minding my own business buying some tomatoes and you've decided to talk to me.

7. 'It's not very ladylike to frown!' This may not happen to my gentleman readers but is a fairly frequent occurrence in my life. I'm often told I'll be more attractive if I smile, if I look like I'm having fun. That a 'lady' shouldn't show her emotions in the way that I do. But you know what? In years gone but women weren't allowed to own property or vote. We can now. And I can look as damn miserable as I want. And this particular comment has the added frisson of passive aggression by suggesting very subtly that I should make more of an effort to be attractive. And if you tell me that Gillian Anderson is going to be in my local supermarket I will. Until then please leave me, and my face, alone.

8. 'Life goes on!' Oh god, does it? Really? Do I need to keep doing this day after day? I'd really rather not, you know. Thanks for reminding there is literally no end to all of this. That I have another twenty to thirty years of waking up and hating everyone and everything. That's brilliant. You should be a therapist.

9. '*I know how you feel. I was depressed once.*' This is a difficult one as it's generally said by someone lovely who is trying to create some empathy with you. They are trying to share their experiences to make you feel better and create a connection to puncture the cloud that's settled around you. The thing is that most of us know that other people have had it, but it doesn't help us at that very moment. It's better to just say, 'I have no idea what you're going through'. Because that's truthful, that's real.

10. '*Just go and have a drink/get laid/buy some shoes!*' Sadly, the act of buying a boss new pair of trainers isn't a cure. If it were I'd have 50,000 pairs of cute sports shoes. And the drinking and casual sex is not recommended for people with insecurities or paranoia. It's safer to stay in and watch an episode of *Friends*. The bottom line is that if there was a simple solution to depression there would be no depressed people. I love that people seem to think you can cure depression just by having fun. 'Take two of these tickets to Alton Towers and call me in the morning.'

11. '*Just take a pill!*' I have my own views on medication which I'll expand on in a later chapter but the headline is that you can't just go to the doctor and get a pill that takes it all away. Well you probably can but it would leave you unable to function in the world. Medication can take time to get right, can have side effects that make them difficult to take and, depending on what is causing the depression, make things worse. A shame, but we don't live in *The Matrix*, where you're offered a red or blue pill and disappear into a different world. I wish I could. I'd disappear into the world of *Cagney and Lacey*. That would absolutely cheer me up.

I'm ashamed to say that I have sworn at people who've used some of these trite statements, and I'm sorry that I did. Some very nice human beings have been left thinking that the sweet lady from Radio 4 is a complete bitch. But if you are in the middle of an episode, a bad time, one of the first things that can go is a sense of proportion. And there's anger, a lot of anger, which is just waiting for an easy target to be directed at.

I don't mean to be insulting towards you if you have in the past tried to help someone using some of these phrases. It can be difficult, even if you have been through a period of depression yourself, to understand exactly what the person in front of you is feeling. The sense of frustration when my head is a mess is palpable; if there were an easy solution the past forty-one years of my life would have been an awful lot happier for everyone in my life, including me. You can never know how much effort it can take to put one foot in front of the other, to go out into the world when you think that the world hates you. Painting on a smile and pretending everything is OK doesn't solve any problems, it just makes them worse.

The only solution is to ask questions and listen, *really listen* to what someone says to you. So next time you're tempted to tell someone to cheer up, or get over it, or smile, why not say something different? Why not ask, 'How are you?' Simple. Just one question that's not passive aggressive or patronising or loaded with emotion. How are you?

'How. Are. You?'

Of course, if you just ask the one question over and over again the conversation is going to get sticky fairly quickly but make sure you are prepared to listen. And in the same way as I have a list of unhelpful statements to make to a depressed person, there are just as many things you can say which might just help someone who's having a tough time.

'I'm here for you.' Said with feeling, this is one of the most incredible things that I have ever heard. Imagine someone sitting next to you, looking you straight in the eye and saying, 'I'm here for you if you want to cry/laugh/watch TV/eat chocolate/drink/run away. I'm here for you no matter what.' How amazing is that? And how simple.

'What can I do to help?' This might sound a bit corporate but there are times when friends are so afraid to offend that they do nothing proactive at all. I often just want a hug, or a cup of tea, or a nice biscuit. A couple of years ago, when I was embarking on my first tour, I had over a hundred dates to book travel and accommodation for, and the enormity of the task just became too much for me. I ended up letting my head become overwhelmed by administration to the extent that I didn't see an end to what was required. So when my wife said, 'Can I help you?' I could have wept with joy. Of course, I had to let go of my control freak ways and actually let someone take some of the load off me, but as soon as I did, a weight was lifted from my shoulders. Help might not be required, but it's nice to let a person know that you're there if assistance is required.

'I believe you. I will listen to you.' Affirmation that what's happening is real is wonderful. That someone else has noticed the change in mood, or simply that you're not yourself. Not being dismissed and instead being believed can help make the condition real. And that's the first step in getting better. Knowing that there is someone who can listen to you can change everything.

'What can we do about it?' Having a partner in crime is a great thing. Someone to talk about Google research, to bitch about a therapist or sit in the doctor's waiting room for you. When it becomes 'we' instead of 'me', any problems automatically become less terrifying. Sometimes lethargy can overwhelm me when I'm depressed, and someone pushing me when I can't do it myself is so important.

'I'm not going to run away.' One of my constant fears is that people will leave me because I'm such a nightmare to be around. And, to be fair, paranoid, depressed, self-obsessed Calman isn't the most pleasant of people at times. Knowing that someone is determined to stick with me no matter what is one of the most comforting things that I can ever hear.

'You are important. You matter.' Telling a friend that they're not as worthless as they believe they are is crucial. They might not believe you initially, but keep saying it until they do.

Finally, I have one other trick that helps me when I'm feeling low. I stand with my hands on my hips, head up, back straight, like a superhero. Genuine scientific research has shown that standing in a powerful position can almost trick the brain into believing that you are a high power individual. Some mornings when I wake up feeling down, I'll stand for ten minutes in my Superman pose and it can genuinely change my mood. If you have a friend who is feeling down, why not be their sidekick? Be a superhero with a friend. You'll both feel fabulous.

CHAPTER 4

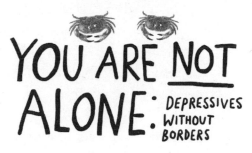

YOU ARE NOT ALONE: DEPRESSIVES WITHOUT BORDERS

I hope that I've established quite firmly that I properly have depression. I don't just have episodes of being a bit down, or normal feelings of self-doubt; they're debilitating episodes that can paralyse me for days. My feelings are so serious that I've even been known to go to the doctor about it, which is a sure sign that something really bad is going on. I'm old fashioned about the medical profession, and was brought up not to bother my GP about frippery, a personality trait which has at times had potentially disastrous consequences for my physical and mental health. Last summer I was walking through Edinburgh and felt something go into my eye. I ignored it, as you do, but after a few days thought I should probably get someone to look at my injury, as there was a very definite black dot visible in the white of my eyeball. I went to my optician first who took one look, shrugged his shoulders and said, 'I have no idea what that is.' How very reassuring. At least he was honest. By way of providing some assistance he told me that I needed to go to the eye hospital, at which point I panicked and implemented my tried and tested emergency health plan:

'Ignore it and eventually it will go away. Or you'll die. Either way, no need to bother anyone.'

So, as you do when told to go straight to a hospital, I waited another four days before finally dragging myself to the speciality clinic, of course I did. It was only when I found myself sitting in the waiting room with fifty other patients, each and every one oozing and weeping from their faces, that I started to become concerned. In fact I started crying. When the doctor called me to the treatment room she was faced with a hysterical woman apologising for being an idiot. She greeted me by saying:

'Word on the street is you have something in your eye.'

Bless her. She was an Ophthalmological Spiderman. She calmly informed me that I had a large piece of metal embedded in my peeper which had, due to the amount of time I'd left it, started working its way into my eyeball. I fully expected to be given some sort of anaesthetic, then gently wheeled into an operating theatre where a team of highly trained surgeons would delicately remove the object. Instead, from a drawer she pulled out what appeared to be a knitting needle to ping it out (which she did) and made me promise that I would never leave it that late again to seek treatment. I apologised twenty or so more times, hugged her inappropriately and skipped out of the clinic wearing a rather fetching eye patch. It wasn't a pirate eye patch, disappointingly, but I drew my own skull and crossbones on it in pen.

Of course, it's easy to ignore symptoms but it doesn't help in the long run. Not least because it can make you feel like you're the only person in the world who is going through what you are. But you're not. Just because something feels tremendously complex doesn't mean that it's not also tremendously common.

The first and most important step is to realise, and admit, that you have depression. It sounds pretty simple but as I've already confessed it can be a very frightening thing to acknowledge. But let me reassure you, once you do accept how you feel you'll be part of the most excellent club in the world. And I should know. When I was twenty I joined the Spice Girls Fan Club, which I thought at the time was a band of likeminded people that couldn't be topped. I was wrong.

You don't get a badge or a membership card just for being sad, but you will have a bond with people all over the world. Don't worry, it's still quite an exclusive organisation and there are entry requirements, although there's no official ceremony when you join. Sorry. Maybe you could listen to some Leonard Cohen to celebrate.

All you need to be part of Depressives Without Borders (might need to work on the name) is to have some sort of mental health condition. I know, I know! You're all excited to join us, but how do you know if you have the right stuff? As I said at the start of this book, I am not medically qualified, but I will attempt to set out some of the most common symptoms of depression through the medium of depression bingo. Shout 'Citalopram!' if you recognise any of them, then send a stamped addressed envelope to the United Nations. You can find the postcode on the Internet.

- One of the key symptoms is the persistent nature of the way you're feeling. Everyone goes through times of feeling unhappy but if you're down for weeks or months then it's possible you may be actually depressed. Keep a note of how long you've felt the way you do to help diagnosis. You don't get extra points for being a hero in DWB. If you bring cake to meetings you might get some extra respect though.

- Sadness, hopelessness and losing interest in things you used to enjoy can be the way that the condition manifests itself. Changes in the way that you perceive life can be indicative that you're more than just a bit annoyed at life.

- I often have feelings of extreme anxiety when I have a spell of depression, and it's very common to find that your stress levels shoot through the roof. Everyone feels that horrible sense of dread on a Monday morning, but do you have that every day?

- Sleep patterns can often be a clear indicator that something is wrong. Feeling tired but being unable to sleep. Loss of appetite and general aches and pains can be physical symptoms that something is wrong up in the head.

- Avoiding contact with friends and family (more than usual).

- Being irritable (more than usual).

- Feeling tearful (more than usual).

- And, of course, thoughts of suicide or self-harm. I will say this throughout this book but if you ever feel like hurting yourself get help immediately. Call someone and talk. It's the most important thing you can do.

I am, of course, making light of a serious situation by dressing up the symptoms as a game. Bingo isn't the way to diagnose anything, although I will say that I find it an extremely enjoyable way of passing an evening. Don't listen to anyone who dismisses it as old people's fun; the last time I played bingo the women beside me played with more aggression and speed than the Scotland rugby team at the last Six Nations tournament.

The point is that depression is a slippery sucker and its root causes and symptoms can vary immensely. The Mental Health Foundation states:

- Depression can happen suddenly as a result of physical illness, experiences dating back to childhood, unemployment, bereavement, family problems or other life-changing events.

- Examples of chronic illnesses linked to depression include heart disease, back pain and cancer. Pituitary damage, a treatable condition that frequently follows head injuries, may also lead to depression.

- Sometimes, there may be no clear reason for your depression but, whatever the original cause, identifying what may affect how you feel and the things that are likely to trigger depression is an important first step.

The foundation also, correctly, points out that there are several types of depression, namely mild depression, major depression, bipolar disorder, post-natal depression and seasonal affective disorder. New research is uncovering more theories about the condition all the time, partly because SO MANY PEOPLE HAVE IT!

It pervades society in an almost incomprehensible way; when you start delving into the research it would be a surprise to meet someone who hasn't had depression at some point. Again, the Mental Health Foundation has provided some statistics to put it in perspective. According to their research, about a quarter of the population will experience some kind of mental health problem in the course of a year. IN A YEAR! Research indicates that women are more likely to have been treated for a mental health problem than men. That doesn't, of course, mean that men aren't suffering from it, it just means that women may have been treated for it. Most worryingly for me, about 10 per cent of children have a mental health problem at any one time and only one in ten prisoners has **no** mental disorder.

The UK also has one of the highest rates of self-harm in Europe, and it's certainly my experience from speaking to fellow sufferers that 'cutting' is increasingly common. I've already said that I've done it in the past and know people who are still doing it. In fact, while writing this book, I started chatting to friends in a way that I haven't before, and a remarkable number of them have been depressed and even more of them have taken medication for it, of some kind, at one point or another. They'd never admitted it before, but then again I suppose I'd never asked.

Almost every day, in the newspapers, you'll find a discussion of the treatment of mental health in the UK, mostly focusing on the fact that the NHS is overwhelmed and underfunded in this area. Of course, the truth is that most of the NHS is overwhelmed and underfunded, and difficult choices are being made about all sorts of treatment areas, leading to criticism and scare stories in broadsheets and tabloids alike.

The political problem is that mental health services are often treated as different from physical health treatments. In fact, it was only in late 2014 that Nick Clegg announced that treatment of depression and other conditions would be brought into line with physical illnesses with the introduction of waiting time standards. Prior to this, in simplistic terms, if you had a cancer diagnosis there were clear guidelines about the time in which you should receive appointments for treatment; the same was not the case for mental health. This policy change also included specific provision in England and Wales (health is a devolved matter in Scotland) for psychiatric services in acute hospitals, so that those presenting in a crisis situation at A & E departments could get the help they need.

It's progress but, and this won't come as a surprise to anyone, it's simply not enough. I truly and firmly believe that the NHS, and the doctors and nurses that work in it, are some of the most dedicated and wonderful professionals you will ever find, but obstacles can be put in your way. I've had a range of GPs in my time, who have ranged from tremendously helpful and sympathetic to clearly tired and annoyed and not really that bothered. Some primary care practitioners will immediately suggest a talking therapy, some will hand you a prescription and a pat on the back.

One question that's often asked of me when I declare my membership of DWB is: 'What tablets do you take for it?' So I should be absolutely clear with you and declare that I have never taken pills for my depression. That's simply my choice and I would never be disparaging about the use of medication to control symptoms. I know many people who have been greatly helped by a daily pill or two and would swear by the change that they've made, and, as with everything in relation to mental health, if it works for you then congratulations and best of luck. It's just my personal belief that I need to deal with the root of my problems, namely my own lack of self-confidence and general feeling of self-hatred.

However, in case any of you break into my house (please don't), I should confess that I do have a well-stocked cupboard in my bathroom filled with Diazepam. But that's not for the Crab of Hate, it's to help with my horrific fear of flying.

Every so often I go to my GP for a refill of my happy pills to help me get on a plane (I'm like a tiny B.A. Baracus), and recently I was given a small insight into the way that people react when they know you're on medication. I went to the chemist and, prior to handing the prescription over, had a nice chat with the pharmacist about this and that. She recognised me from the television and was asking what it was like to be on *QI* and whether it was intimidating being on such an intelligent show. I replied that it was a lot of fun and everyone was tremendously welcoming, etc., etc. We were getting on like a house of fire and I fully expected us to swap phone numbers and go on a caravan holiday together in the summer.

Then I handed over the little piece of paper that contained the magic words 'Diazepam'. Her face changed like she was in a cartoon. She looked at me with what I can only describe as pity. She stopped talking immediately and turned her back. After filling the box with the magic tablets she passed them to me, took my hand and said, 'Good luck.' I wanted to say 'It's OK, I just hate flying', but I didn't. I was so embarrassed she thought that the woman she'd watched on *QI* was mental that I scurried out of the shop.

That fairly recent encounter is partly why I'm emptying my head in this book. I know how embarrassed you might be about admitting to a stranger how you're feeling. I know how horrific it is to build up the courage to say to a doctor how bad things are. To talk about the deepest darkest thoughts you may have been having. But be confident. This is your head after all, and they want you to get better. Don't be put off. Don't feel embarrassed. Imagine how many other times a GP has heard someone trying to explain how they feel. We all want to feel special, but, remember, one in four people has struggled with mental health issues.

The perception of depression is getting better with more and more well-known people speaking publicly about their struggles. Even politicians are willing to be more open about the fact that they have sought help from professionals. I often find that it helps people who haven't been through something understand what we're going through if they can hook it to someone they like on the television.

'You're depressed? Like that nice man Stephen Fry? Oh I like him. He's so funny.'

Of course, the portrayal of the condition in the media isn't necessarily always the most positive. The glee with which journalists report murder, mayhem and disorder by some with mental health problems feeds into the fear that the general public have, and also the fear that those of us who live with it have. But we're a gang that's been around since the dawn of time and, let's face it, barring a miracle, we're not going away.

You're not alone. Far from it. If the statistics are even partially correct, many more people you know than you can possibly imagine are probably feeling the same way you do. Sadly, there's no handshake to help you identify yourself, no uniform or special sticker for your car. But they're out there, like you, part of the invisible millions. Imagine the Depressives Without Borders Christmas Party! It would be a hoot.

CHAPTER 5
I'M *NOT* MAD BECAUSE I'M GAY:
COMING OUT AND MARRIAGE

ONE of the most common initial diagnoses for the cause of my depression is my sexuality. Some people have even directly suggested that I'm a bit mad because I'm gay. *'Get her a date with a boy and she'll be fine! Job done.'* And believe me when I say that I am really gay. If sexuality is a sliding scale I'm way over to the left, well beyond Jodie Foster and Ellen DeGeneres.

But what's the connection between the Crab of Hate and my love of women? Well, I always knew I was different from other girls of my age, that I had a different way of thinking about life even if I didn't equate it with my sexuality at that point. When my classmates played with dolls I played with an Action Man tank. Rather against the grain, I enjoyed wearing sensible Clark's shoes and my idea of dressing up was wearing pinstriped dungarees. But the final nail in the coffin of any idea my parents might have that I was just like every other little girl came in a rather unexpected way.

I was between the ages of five and eight. I can't be more specific as I don't have very good recall for dates, a flaw which is going to make my autobiography as precise as measuring the volume of a swimming pool with a thimble. Anyway, I was certainly younger than ten years old and, like most children in the area, I attended my local church. The biggest event of the year, as you might expect, was the nativity play, and at the nativity play the most important role for any young girl was, of course, Mary. Every year a new girl was appointed Jesus's mother, an ever-evolving conveyor belt of the cream of the crop of Sunday school attendees. Speculation was rife as to who would get the coveted role. You know the firestorm of excitement that accompanies a new *Doctor Who*? It was just like that. The other girls in my Sunday school class were beside themselves at the thought of being chosen, whereas I was nonchalant. I was blonde at that time and unbelievably cute, but I didn't think I'd be in the frame due to my constant questioning of the scriptures and my penchant for wearing my *Star Wars* stormtrooper costume to church.

Then the day came. I was summoned to the office of the head of the Sunday school and given some shocking news. They asked me, Susan Calman, to play the part of Mary. I was distraught. I ran out of the church hall as delicately as my stormtrooper outfit would allow (the plastic joints were fairly inflexible). I was in tears when my mother collected me, which was to be honest not an unusual state of affairs. Just as I am a tearful adult, I was always a tearful child and so to find me hysterical was not an immediate cause for concern. However, even my parents were shocked when they finally coaxed the cause of my concern out of me. 'I don't want to be the Virgin Mary!' I wailed. 'But why?' they pleaded. I was unaware at the time, but being the parents of the girl chosen to be Mary had some form of social cachet, like having a really impressive racehorse. But I was firm. I knew exactly why I didn't want to play the mother of the Baby Jesus in the Scotstoun Parish Church nativity play and I told them. 'I don't want to be the Virgin Mary because I'll have to kiss a boy!'

And that was it. If ever a clue was needed as to how I would turn out it happened early in December 1978. Or 1979. And so it transpired that little girl with the dungarees who didn't want to kiss a boy in church grew up to be a larger girl with dungarees who still didn't want to kiss a boy in church.

I must tell you the outcome of that story. When the church was told by my embarrassed parents they were, understandably perhaps, slightly annoyed. However, as a compromise I was allowed to be the Angel Gabriel. A part much better suited to a small child with a god complex.

It turns out that there was a pretty valid reason why I didn't want to kiss a boy. You see, I wasn't so much a friend of Dorothy as that I wanted to go out with Dorothy, spend our Saturdays at Ikea and recycle a lot. Maybe adopt some cats and listen to K.D. Lang while carving wood. I kept my feelings secret for many years (of course I did!) until it became quite frankly tiring to continue to do so. I was a master of talking without specificity about my activities when I went home for Christmas, of speaking in gender-neutral terms like 'this person', 'they' and 'someone'. I had to come clean and tell my family the truth.

I eventually came out to my parents on my twentieth birthday. It was an extra present for them; there was no need to thank me. If you haven't been through this yourself you may not know that coming out is very much a competitive sport for many gay people. It's like a game of top trumps of who's had the worst time. 'Oh, you got shot in the head, you win.' I was so used to the horrific stories that my friends had relayed that I was a tad more confrontational than perhaps should have been when I came out. I remember it very clearly. My mother was watching *Inspector Morse* while sitting down doing the ironing. Which incidentally I didn't know was odd until I moved in with my first girlfriend and said I was going to do the ironing and sat down. Apparently most people do it standing up. Strange.

I remember walking in and saying to my mother, 'I've got something to say to you old woman and you can't say anything until I've said what I have to say, right? Mum, I'm a blahhhhH!' I couldn't say it myself which was a major problem. 'Mum I'm a, ahhhh, Mum I'm a, eeeeeeh, Mum I'm a gay!' She carried on ironing and said very calmly, 'Oh well, you never did like boys did you?' It was almost like she'd been paying attention. She said, 'Would you like me to tell your father?' and I said, 'Yeah, you tell him. You tell him what I am.' And I went home and sat in the dark, smoking Gauloises and imagining what it would be like to be an orphan – because that's what was going to happen to me. The phone went and my father said, 'Your mother's told me,' and I said, 'Yeah and what've you got to say about it, eh?' And he said, 'It doesn't matter.' And I thought, *You bastard. How am I meant to get a book deal out of supportive parents!*

I am entirely comfortable with my sexuality, in fact at times it's the only thing that I am happy with. My depression has never been caused by any feelings of guilt, or fear that how I feel is in any way wrong. That's not to say that it hasn't had an impact on my mental health, mainly because there have been times when I have been told that what I feel is wrong. The world in which I grew up was not one that was accepting of the LGBTIQ community, and all around me were signals that I was entering a dark and dangerous world that would mean I was ostracised from normality. Looking back at archive footage from the seventies, eighties and even the nineties, the venom with which even the word 'homosexuality' was said by news anchors and pressure groups was the same tone used when discussing 'perverts'. Many in society thought that was what we were, and while I had no problem with my feelings, I started to think I wasn't normal – I was the 'other'.

You may not know this but as a lesbian with mental health issues I am in one of the highest risk groups on television you will ever encounter. If you watch a TV show and a character wears sensible shoes and feels a bit down quite a lot, then she will either a) get murdered b) kill someone c) kill themselves d) kidnap a child e) burn something down f) all of the above. In fact, some writers seem to believe that if you have a lady gay character in a show they automatically have to be mad in some way. Which doesn't reflect reality of course. I have many heterosexual friends who are far more disturbed than any lesbian I've met. But it suits a traditional narrative that to be gay you have to be, in some way, a little bit wrong.

It's not such a strange connection to make given the way that some in the medical profession have treated homosexuality in the not too distant past. I distinctly recall while at university and studying forensic medicine that the textbook we were given still included homosexuality as a sexual perversion and mental illness. Those showing unnatural inclinations could be classed as having a mental disorder and undoubtedly some of my community ended up in asylums and subjected to aversion therapies because of who they were attracted to. For many years, even up until the late 1970s, many believed that it could be treated by the science of medicine, even on the NHS. Shock treatments were commonly used to try to alter patients' sexuality, and treatment in psychiatric hospitals was often brutal and violent. And there is no question that there are still some in the world who genuinely believe that being attracted to someone of the same sex can be treated and cured. The issue isn't going away, on 21 October 2015 the Education Secretary and Minister for Women and Equalities, Nicky Morgan, said that 'gay cures' should be eradicated. In pinknews.co.uk she was reported to say:

'I was shocked to discover that one in ten social and healthcare staff have heard colleagues express the belief that someone can be cured of being gay.'

While attitudes are changing, when I was growing up there was far more of a belief that homosexuality was a disease, so I was depressed and gay. Some might say I had a double whammy of mental illness, although the two don't cancel each other out.

That's not to say that there isn't a high level of depression and mental illness in the gay community. In fact some studies have shown that suicide in the LGBTIQ community is higher than in a comparative section of the heterosexual community. LGBTIQ support charity Metro, in a survey of sixteen- to twenty-four-year-olds across the UK, found that:

42 per cent of young LGBTIQ people have sought medical help for anxiety or depression

52 per cent of young LGBTIQ people report self-harm either now or in the past

44 per cent of young LGBTIQ people have considered suicide

Alarming statistics, and many have speculated as to the cause. As I said before, I don't believe that the fact that I'm gay caused my depression, but I'm pretty sure that some of the more negative parts of my lifestyle didn't help. These days there are new-fangled things called 'computers' and 'the Internet', and it might be difficult for some young people to understand, but there was a time when it was perfectly possible to feel like the only gay person in the world. I'm pretty sure that there were some magazines or periodicals out there, but when you're not brave enough to admit to yourself how you feel, you're quite unlikely to admit it to a sales assistant in WH Smith. In addition, magazines for the gays were almost always placed on the top shelf alongside the pornographic magazines, which was not only embarrassing but because of my small stature logistically very difficult to reach.

You may comfort yourself by thinking that such prejudice doesn't exist today, and you would be very wrong. Almost every day I encounter the perception of gay people that we're obsessed with sex and that the general population should be protected from our foul sinful lifestyle. And I find evidence of this on an almost daily basis. Most companies with Wi-Fi employ a filtering system to prevent people doing things they shouldn't on their network; that's fair enough, it's simply part of being a responsible employer/company. But these filters also reinforce a long held prejudice about the gay community that might make you think we're still living in the 1970s.

Anyone who follows me on Twitter will know I spend a large proportion of my life on trains. Mostly I can be found on a Virgin train from Glasgow to London Euston: in fact, I'm down south so often that I spend more time with the crew on these trains than I do with my own family. Something my family is probably very grateful for. As with other equivalent providers, Virgin offers a Wi-Fi service for passengers. It's of varying quality, of course. At times I think a carrier pigeon would beat my email, but birds get angry when you put them in a laptop bag, so I'll stick with iffy Wi-Fi for now.

On one of my many trips down south in 2013, I was sent a tweet about an event taking place as part of Glasgay, the successful LGBTIQ arts festival held in my home town. When I tried to access the website I found this message.

- The webpage you are attempting to access is restricted.

- This Wi-Fi service provides some limitations on access to the Internet. We have therefore restricted access to certain websites considered to be inappropriate or malicious.

I tried again, but this was clearly more than a simple malfunction of the service. I tweeted Virgin Trains, was given a number to call and spoke to an adviser. I was told that the site was blocked as it was classified as 'porn'. He immediately unblocked the site and, the last time I checked, it is now accessible on their services. I asked the tech operator directly if it had been blocked because the website contained the word 'gay' and he assured me it wasn't.

I found that position difficult to believe given the content of the website. Glasgay.co.uk contains nothing pornographic or offensive that I can see. And it turns out that it's not an isolated incident. According to others who contacted me on Twitter, more than one other transport operator had similarly blocked the Glasgay website.

It seems that there are automatic filters in use by some providers that are rather overzealous in their application of criteria to distinguish what is considered 'offensive'. Internet filtering is a software process that automatically blocks access to sites considered 'unsuitable' for viewing.

I wrote a column about the issue for *Diva* magazine who contacted the companies involved for comment before the publication went to print. Virgin Trains slightly misunderstood the question as they said that there was no problem as the website was accessible. Which it was. Because I got it unblocked. ScotRail sent the following comment:

- We're sorry that it appears that some websites have been by unwittingly blocked by automatic filtering software. We are glad that this has been brought to our attention – and are working to fix this issue by proactively over-riding restrictions on dozens more websites.

Without sitting and searching for every publication that contains the word 'gay', it's difficult to know the extent of the problem, but it seems to me there's a possibility an assumption is being made the word 'gay' is a neon sign to offensive content. Which is, at the very least, an old-fashioned and bigoted notion. Of course, it may all just be a weird coincidence, but at the moment it looks like LGBTIQ websites have been dumped in a barrel marked 'dodgy'. I'm sure some people might find any representation of our community offensive, but they're not the majority. We all know that 'gay' doesn't automatically mean a website will be chock full of filth and sex. We do look at other sites, as my Internet history proves. *Searches for cats in evening gowns*

I have also found the same problem in hotels, with other transport companies and in free Wi-Fi spots in coffee shops. I was so concerned about this filtering of innocuous websites that when I was on tour the first thing I always did when I checked into a hotel was ascertain what their web filtering policy was. Actually the first thing I did was check under the bed, in the wardrobe and the shower in case anyone was hiding in the room, but right after that I would check the Internet. And, more often than not, the results were upsetting.

For example, I was staying at a hotel in Inverness and tried to log on to the Stonewall website to check an auction that was running. It's a source of some embarrassment to me that I was checking how much someone was willing to pay for, well, me. I'd been asked to offer a prize to support the organisation, but having little on the go at the time all I could offer was me. Not in a sexual sense, I love Stonewall but don't believe prostitution is the way to raise awareness of LGBTIQ issues. Being an intellectual, the offer I'd made was to attend a book group and chat about whatever text they were interested in. It was only after I offered to do that that the panic set in. Imagine putting yourself out there to be bid on! What if no one wanted me? I was filled with some urgency as I tried to check whether or not I had to phone my wife and demand that she paid money to spend time with me. I couldn't get into the Stonewall website as it was (surprise!) blocked as porn. I called reception but was met with the usual excuse that they outsourced their web work and couldn't do anything about it. I lodged a formal complaint and followed up with an email, although I don't know if they did anything about it. Now, even though it wasn't the best hotel in the world, I'm going to have to stay there next time I'm up north. To check if anything has changed. Sometimes being a campaigner can be very uncomfortable.

It makes me feel desperately sad that those kinds of attitudes still pervade large parts of society. What kind of message does it send to someone growing up today that when they try to access an innocuous news site, or an organisation that promotes LGBTIQ equality, it's blocked? That to 'normal' people everything I do is probably to do with sex. It's an obsession from the ignorant spread by the stupid. It's why, in 2016 gay people are still attacked in the street, suffer discrimination in employment and have to fight for equality.

I'm pretty sure that being gay but not really knowing what that meant contributed to my depression when I was younger. Isolation can be a key trigger to the start of a depressive period and, in the formative years, when friendships are made and 'normal' relationships are being discussed, being the only gay at school can make matters much worse. I went to the school discos, I bought the puffball skirts and the batwing cardigans, but I just couldn't make any connections with my peer group. As a result, I suspect I was rather more emotionally immature than some of my contemporaries, and found it difficult to make meaningful friendships until far later in my life than some did.

Fundamentally, even though I didn't quite know what I was, and neither did the people in my class, it was clear that I was different. These days, being gay is something that most children just accept. My little niece who is three at the time of writing is delighted to tell me that she plays a game called 'Auntie Susan and Auntie Lee' at nursery with her best friend. When I asked her what that meant she said that they dress as princesses and look after the babies. It's not a particularly realistic game, but bless her.

I didn't feel I could talk at home about how I felt and I didn't feel that I had any contemporaries in whom I could confide. It was still an era where limp wrists were a sign of being a poof, and dykes were those awful women who chained themselves to the fences at Greenham Common. I was also unfortunate to grow up during the time of Section 28/Clause 28 which was passed in 1988 and stated that a local authority:

- shall not intentionally promote homosexuality or publish material with the intention of promoting homosexuality

or

- promote the teaching in any maintained school of the acceptability of homosexuality as a pretended family relationship

You can argue, and many have, that it didn't stop schools from talking about homosexuality, that it wouldn't have stopped me talking about how I felt, but imagine watching the news and knowing that politicians like Lord Somers were saying:

- One has only to look through the entire animal world to realise that it is abnormal. In any case, the clause as it stands does not prohibit homosexuality in any form; it merely discourages the teaching of it. When one is young at school one is very impressionable and may just as easily pick up bad habits as good habits.

A few years ago I had what would kindly be described as a discussion with a man who was a teacher about the time that I was growing up. He stated quite clearly that Section 28/Clause 28 had absolutely no effect on how he taught and that we gays should just get over it. I calmly explained that unless you were gay it is difficult to understand how the use of the law to talk about 'the acceptability of homosexuality' might have made those of us who were gay feel like outsiders and perverts.

In the year 2000, when attempts were made to repeal the legislation in Scotland, Brian Souter funded the 'Keep the Clause' campaign. I clearly recall seeing the posters and the articles about what children should be taught regarding what was a normal and acceptable life to lead. The newly formed Scottish Parliament voted to get rid of the legislation and that action started a new chapter for my community in Scotland. But I can never forget that time, and what some people believed that I, and my fellow gays, represented to them. A threat. A perversion. A danger.

While as a society we have all moved on greatly from those dark times of ignorance, there are still some practical issues that can continue to make me feel like an outsider to society and means that the feelings of isolation persist. I got married last year, properly married, but only after a debate (which is still ongoing in some countries) about whether I should have the right to marry.

The propaganda about equal marriage was, and remains, astonishing. I read in the papers that if gay people were allowed to get married it would be a shame on Scotland. I'll tell you now the most shameful thing I've ever done. Don't get excited, it's not like that. I once was in Burger King and – I don't know how I did this, I doubt I'll ever be able to do it again – I opened a sachet of tomato ketchup with my teeth, squeezed it against my cheek and it squirted onto the jacket of a man sitting across the restaurant from me. And I never said a thing. That is the most shameful thing I've ever done.

The fact that a large group of predominantly straight people were allowed to sit in the House of Commons and discuss whether or not I had the right to a wedding was offensive, as were many of the arguments put forward. Firstly, there's the argument that the Bible prohibits it, well I dismiss that quite easily. The Bible says a lot of things that we no longer pay attention to. Like you can beat a woman to death with a piece of cheese on a Sunday. Something like that anyway. The second argument is the moral slippery slope argument. In fact, one of my favourite stories about the whole equal marriage issue was when the floods happened in England. The newspapers published a story where a member of the clergy said that the floods were a direct result of people like me wanting to get married, eroding the morality of this country to such an extent that god was punishing us with rain. What a pile of nonsense. Gays like summer too!

American preacher Luke Robinson also suggested Hurricane Sandy was our fault as well. I never knew I had so much power, I'm like Storm from the X-Men. One particularly fabulous member of the House of Lords suggested that if gay people were allowed to marry the next thing that would happen would be people being able to marry their pets. Which I would be in favour of, actually. My cat is very handsome.

But it's an argument worth thinking about. If people like me are allowed to marry, before we know it, the morals of society will erode to such an extent that the general public will no longer be able to trust people. People like, I don't know, politicians, bankers and the clergy. Because they've always been so trustworthy, haven't they? Of course they have.

The reality is that no matter how out you might think I am, I still have to come out every day. Booking hotel rooms, appointments for my wife, introducing her to people. And I'm doing that not knowing what the reaction of the person I'm speaking to will be. When I was a young lawyer in Glasgow, I worked in a law firm that, outwardly, was totally fine with my sexuality. But it wasn't. Every year they had a big social event to entertain clients. Solicitors had to attend but they were allowed to bring their significant others to it. I heard through the office grapevine that the partners of the firm had a meeting during which they discussed how they would deal with the situation if I brought a woman to the evening. How they would deal with it? Perhaps make me wear a sign around my neck or ring a bell so that important people knew that there was a homosexual approaching. As it happened, I was single at the time so they clearly thought more of my ability to attract a lady than I did. I did toy, briefly, with finding the tallest, leggiest blonde I could find to come with me and terrify the polite Scottish legal establishment. Looking back I really wish I had.

Even when I perform my stand-up shows, I don't know whether or not someone will have a problem with who I am because of inherent prejudice. On my last UK tour I performed a show that comprised two sections of forty-five minutes each. The first half was, in my view, pretty light on the gay front – with a few references to my wife, but nothing that the Gay Liberation Front would applaud. Despite this, a man in the audience of one particular show was overheard in the interval to ask if the second half was going to be 'less lesbian'. Initially, when I heard what he said, I genuinely started to question just how lesbian I'd been in the first half. I mean I talk about my life and experiences but I don't walk out wearing dungarees and holding a poster of Sue Perkins. I didn't have time to find the gentleman in question after the show to ask him exactly what he meant, and, to be honest, I've been stewing about it ever since. I know that he can have no idea what chain reaction his flippant comment set off in my head.

As I've already admitted, when I was sixteen I was in a very bad place. Now I can think about that time in my life and the positives that it has left me with. And there are some. It's left me with more empathy for those who struggle with their own thoughts and sexuality, but also a strong desire to reach out to people. I'm gay, and if I don't talk about it then I'm still that frightened girl in a hospital unsure of who she was. I know exactly who I am now. And if by talking about it I make people uncomfortable then sod it.

So the answer to that man in the audience is no. I will never be less lesbian. I will always be who I am, on stage, off stage, at the shops, on a train, wherever. I will never be frightened of being who I am. And while I can, I'll make sure no one else feels that isolated. I'm also toying with calling my show next year 'Susan Calman: Less Lesbian'. Maybe he'll come and see it, although somehow I doubt it.

There's no question in my mind that being gay can make things more difficult no matter how confident or 'out' I appear in public. If anything, it makes me more proactive about announcing my sexuality. If I rush on stage and talk about being a lesbian, and I'm loud and brash, then I can drown out anyone with outdated or offensive views. Then I won't hear the Crab of Hate whispering in my ear:

> 'They're right you know. You aren't normal. You're an aberration, you're weird, if you just tried harder you could be the same as everyone else'

But I am normal. I'm so normal I'm now married, legally properly married. But the Crab of Hate didn't want me to be, oh no. He hates it when I'm happy. Even when I met the woman I loved, and we'd set the date, he still whispered in my ear the reasons why no one in their right mind would ever take me on. I wrote them down in list form. Of course I did.

Number one. This. The fact that I have a list entitled 'Reasons why no one should marry me'. It's not that normal is it, but I write lists about everything. My wife keeps saying we need to be more spontaneous and I say fine, when? If I go on holiday, I write out my itinerary, laminate it and post it to all the members of my family. My wife says, 'But a holiday is about relaxing,' and I say, 'That's where you're wrong, a holiday is about organisation, we've got half an hour at the Louvre, move, move, move!'

I have some horrific foibles. For example, I hate littering. I spend a lot of time at the window of my tenement property watching the street, looking for litterers. Usually with a cat under my arm, because a second pair of eyes always helps. I didn't think anyone could see me, until quite recently. I was standing at the window and some children were playing football while I was watching *Loose Women*. I need complete silence for that, so I opened the window and shouted, 'Stop having fun!' and they looked up and shouted, 'Run it's the mad cat lady!' Yes it is. I think I have a healthy sense of worry from my mother, you see. She doesn't like driving in the rain, the dark or reversing, so neither do I. When I was younger she told me it was illegal to feed squirrels. I spent a great deal of my life, including time at university, going up to people in parks telling them they were breaking the law. When I got my first job as a solicitor I spent a great deal of time trying to find the relevant squirrel statute. When I couldn't, I phoned her and asked her the origin of the law. She said, 'Oh I probably just made that up, to keep you away from squirrels.'

Number two. When we first discussed getting married, I said that I had only one condition: that I wanted a diamond ring. When I first told my better half she was quite confused as I'm not very materialistic. I said it's not about the bling lady, no. I wanted a diamond ring because of *Hart to Hart*. You see, when I was eight years old I watched an episode of *that show* that's stayed with me for thirty years. If you don't remember *Hart to Hart* you've missed out. Back in the days when we had three channels it was that or *Quincy*. End of. Jonathan and Jennifer Hart were millionaires and when they met, it was murder! They had a little dog called Freeway and a butler called Max.

In the episode that's stayed with me, Jennifer Hart was

trapped in a giant glass box that was slowly filling with poisoned gas. Why? It's irrelevant. Luckily, that very morning, Jonathan Hart had given Jennifer Hart a giant diamond ring and she cut her way out of the glass box with a circular sweep of her arm. Now, I'm a worrier and I've always been concerned that the same thing might happen to me. Some of you may be thinking, that's going too far, that won't happen, it's impossible. Wrong! It's improbable; it's not impossible. And for those of you scoffing, well, you better hope that if you're ever trapped in a giant glass box that's slowly filling with poisoned gas that I'm there. You'll be like, 'We're going to die, we're going to die!' and I'll be like, 'Calm down, I've got this one.'

The point is this. When I explained to my wife that I wanted to spend thousands of pounds on a diamond ring because of *Hart to Hart* she didn't say 'don't be silly' she went: 'OK then.'

Number three. My cats. I love them, I love them, I love them. They've got middle names. Muppet Dollop, Pickle Kylie and Oscar Liberace. And they each have theme tunes that you have to sing when they come into the room. Well, you don't have to, it's not the law. But they get upset if you don't sing to them.

We also have fun dressing up. They love it. Of course it can lead to awkward situations. One day in particular is burned into my brain because of the arrival of the Tesco man. I have very short arms, you see, and so can't carry heavy shopping. And I'm lazy. Anyway, I was preparing for a day of dressing up and getting ready for my shopping. The doorbell rang, I answered it wearing my velour housecoat. The delivery man, much to my chagrin, was insisting on bringing the shopping bags into the house rather than leaving them at the front door as I requested. He kept trying to look over my shoulder and said, 'What's going on?' and I said, 'Just leave it there mate,' and he said, 'What's going on?' and I said, 'Just leave it there mate,' and he said, 'What's going on?' and then he kicked the door open to see three cats dressed in police uniforms. Because it was obviously *Prime Suspect* Day. I was DCI Jane Tennison in a simple navy blue suit with an ivory blouse. The cats were police constables.

Now I doubt you've ever been in the situation where a delivery man is staring at three cats in, if I may be so bold, intricately made police uniforms. Do you know how difficult it is to get epaulettes on a cat? They have no shoulders! Anyway, the man was staring at me, I was staring at him. I thought that the best way to deal with the situation was to pretend that what was happening was perfectly normal and that he was clinically insane. He said, 'What's going on?' and I said, 'It's *Prime Suspect* Day,' he said, '*Prime Suspect* Day?' I said, '*Prime Suspect* Day,' he said '*Prime Suspect* Day? Is that a religious holiday?' I said, 'Yes! Whatever.' The sad thing is that he believed me. If you ever see a Tesco man dressed as a policeman just say '*Prime Suspect* Day?' and I won't feel quite as evil.

Number four on my list of reasons why no one should marry me. I recently mistook a child for a dog. Now this sounds stranger than it actually is. I love dogs, and I love talking to dogs. Especially the ones that you see tied up outside supermarkets. I always take the time to stop and chat to them. I say, 'Hello wee doggy,' and they say, 'Hello Susan!' They always know my name, I don't know how. I was walking along the street and I was rehearsing an argument that I was about to have. I know you might think I'm all assertive but I'm not really. I was walking along the street saying, 'You can stick it, no you can stick it, no you can stick it.' I was on my way to the Vodafone shop. They had sold me a turkey, a phone that seemed incapable of phoning, which was very inconvenient. I kept going in and saying, 'Give me a new phone,' but they say, 'We can't we're just the Vodafone shop,' which seemed like a tautologous argument. I snapped one day, it was like Michael Douglas in *Falling Down*. I walked into the shop and said, 'Give me a new phone!' and they said, 'We can't we're just the Vodafone shop,' and I said, 'If you don't give me a new phone I'll chain myself to your desk. I look like a twelve-year-old child. Do you want people walking past your branch and seeing a twelve-year-old child chained to a desk?' And they gave me a new phone. Anyway, I was walking down the street rehearsing my argument 'You can stick it, no you can stick it, no you can stick it' and I saw a wee doggy and I thought, *That'll cheer me up*. So I said, 'Hello wee doggy!' and it turned round and it was a child.

In my defence there's a fashion for dressing children like animals, you'll have seen the costumes in the shops. What I'm saying is that it was entrapment. Now, have you ever been in the situation where you've called a parents' pride and joy, their child, an animal? It's awkward. I stood as the mother stared at me and I thought, *You're a comedian Susan, think of something to get out of this. Think of something funny*. And I'm not proud, but all I could think of to say was this: 'I'm sorry, I'm very drunk,' and I walked away. Now I always check that it's a real dog.

Number five on my list. I have two black hairs that grow out of my chin. It looks like a stick man has jumped on a trampoline and become embedded in there. It's something that happens to ladies as they get older. You go to bed one night perfectly normal and wake up in the morning as David Bellamy. Here's a tip for the gents reading this: you'll often see women in cars stroking their chins looking really thoughtful. They're not thinking about anything other than, *How the hell did I miss that this morning*. I also have one white hair that grows out of the centre of my forehead. Kind of like a unicorn. I try and keep that under control but will often miss it, leaving me to wonder why I ever ask for assistance in shops. With my home-made fishing rod I can reach anything myself.

The last reason why no one should marry me is a very serious one. Anyone who's in a long-term relationship will know that one of the joys is that you know exactly what to do to the other person to make them as angry as is humanly possible in thirty seconds. Sometimes that's all you have left. I've been having an argument with my better half for twelve years. Same argument, twelve years. Some people suggest that I should give it up, let it go. But you know what that is? That's losing. And you know what that means? Losing forever.

I'm hoping if I write down the argument you will read it, agree with me, and she will be defeated.

My better half and I were watching a television programme called *The West Wing*. You don't need to have seen it to understand the story, suffice to say it's about the American political system. We watched it and we were having a light-hearted discussion, you know the type of light-hearted discussion you might have with your beloved after watching a television show. I said, 'Darling, if you were in *The West Wing* who would you be?' Light-hearted. She said, 'CJ,' and I said 'That's lovely darling, you're so very beautiful.' Then she said, 'Who would you be?' Now, because I'm short and I have a Napoleon complex, I said, 'President of the United States.' Without missing a beat, without blinking, she said, 'But you can't be Susan, you're not American.' I thought I had misheard and said, 'Darling, we're having a light-hearted conversation about *The West Wing*. I'd be President of the United States,' and she, very calmly, repeated, 'But you can't be Susan, you're not American.' I said, 'Darling, we're having a light hearted discussion,' and she said, 'Don't get upset Susan, I can't do anything about it, neither of us are elected members of Congress or the Senate, I can't change the law.' I said, 'Darling, we're having a light-hearted discussion about *The West Wing*. When we had a light-hearted discussion about *Battlestar Galactica*, I didn't say you couldn't be Admiral Adama because they was no such thing as a spaceship!' And she said, 'Calm down sweetie, you're not the first person to feel like this. It must be how Arnold Schwarzenegger felt when he wanted to run for president.'

For twelve years I've been trying to get her to say that I can be President of the United States. I get her drunk to try and get her to say it. A friend of mine walked into a pub in Glasgow recently and saw me screaming like a madwoman, 'WILL YOU LET ME BE PRESIDENT OF THE UNITED STATES!'

But I need to win the argument. So I've done something. Some people think I've gone too far. I say not far enough. I've changed my will. There is now only one provision that matters. And that is, when I die and I am buried, my tombstone must be inscribed with the words: 'Susan Calman: President of the United States!'

And I will be dead, but I will have won.

She still married me though, despite all my foibles and my problems and the fact that there's always a silent partner in the marriage in the form of the Crab of Hate. The point is that depression is not, and has never been, homophobic. It doesn't care who you sleep with or who you marry. I'm definitely not mad because I'm gay, although sometimes my depression isn't helped by society's attitude to what is a 'normal' way of life. We're all the same when it comes to sadness, there's no pink branch of Depressives Without Borders. This is one area of life where we're definitely all the same.

CHAPTER 6

TO UNIVERSITY AND BEYOND: STARRING AMY SCHUMER

I tend to split my life into easy-to-understand sections. Partly because it helps me to compartmentalise how I felt at that particular time and move on, but also because it assists me as I try to understand what went right, or more likely wrong. And I'm not going to lie, it'll make it easier for future film-makers to decide the casting for a movie based on my life. Which is the dream of course. To have the life and times of Susan Calman turned into a made-for-TV movie on Channel 5. For any directors reading this, I've compiled what I think is the most appropriate list of actresses who I'm sure would love to be involved in the project:

Young Calman – Taylor Swift
University Calman – Amy Schumer
Lawyer Calman – Kate Winslet
Comedy Calman – Amy Poehler
Older Calman – Helen Mirren

You might think that some of these are odd choices. Far from it. These are plum roles with 'Oscar winning' written all over them. Strangely, all of the women I've nominated to play me are blondes. Something I didn't realise until I'd finished the list. There must be some strange psychological reason for it, because I most certainly do not look good as a blonde. Except when I was a child of course, and my golden locks made me the perfect Mary. In my adult years I bleached my hair once and I can assure you I did not look like Marilyn Monroe. I looked like an aggressive German tennis player who has anger issues.

The most challenging part of those on offer to the Hollywood elite is probably the time I was at university, which will afford the fabulous Amy Schumer a chance to play Calman when everything became brilliant and awful at the same time.

I went to university partly because it was expected of me. I really, really wanted to be a stand-up comedian, but in 1992 if I'd revealed that ambition to my parents I might as well have said I wanted to run away to join the circus. In fact, they would have preferred that because at least when you're a proper clown accommodation comes with the job. It's not that my parents were bad people who didn't want me to fulfil my dreams, far from it, it's just their role was to make sure that I had the best start in life. To them getting a degree and having a career would mean that I could look after myself and be financially secure. They were the first in their family to go on to further education and it's seen as a mark of success if your children follow in your footsteps. I'm not even sure I really knew what I meant by 'wanting to be a comedian'. It was a concept that I threw around in my head like 'wanting to be one of Charlie's Angels' or 'wanting to own France'.

Let me just remind you of what kind of state I was in at this time. I had suffered a bout of depression which had reached a severe level and I'd been hospitalised. My parents were quite rightly concerned about how I would cope away from home, but doing a sensible thing like going to university was a welcome return to normality that everyone needed. I was also pretty convinced that if I could just get away from home and all of the restrictions that I believed it entailed, I could shake off the Crab of Hate who'd become increasingly vocal in my latter days at school.

Except I had a pretty major problem that was standing in my way, namely I had no idea what I wanted to be in life. I'd spent most of my time at school lost in a fog of self-hatred where there was little room for considering the next week, never mind the rest of my life. My depression can often take the form of mental and physical lethargy, robbing me of any ambition or desire to succeed.

At the required meeting with my careers teacher it was suggested that the best thing for me to do might be to study some form of arts course and maybe become a journalist. What she really meant was 'we don't quite know what to do with you, go and read some books and see if you can't make yourself feel better'. Which made me feel even more like an outsider because I was being treated differently from my contemporaries. If you were in any way academic at my school, the expected career path was to study medicine or law. Just because I was sad sometimes shouldn't mean that I was to be treated any differently from my peers, should it?

Fortunately, the choice was easy because I hated blood, leaving law the only option available to me. Besides, loads of people at my school were going to be lawyers, so why not? And that, stupidly, was the reason I chose to study law, because lots of other people were doing the same.

It's fair to say that in my teenage years I was easily influenced by my peers, hence the perm I got when I was thirteen, closely followed by a perm and streaks I got when I was fourteen, leaving me looking like I'd been attacked by an angry seagull with a Braun Independent.

So I didn't choose to be a lawyer because of a burning desire to right the wrongs of society, or protect those who had no voice. I did it because other people said it would be a good thing to do. Oh, and because it looked good on the television. Of course, my acceptance of the representation of the legal profession on the television as fact left me tremendously disappointed when I finally started working as a solicitor and it was nothing whatso-ever like *Ally McBeal*.

My only real idea of what university would be like was from a) watching *University Challenge* and b) watching *Chariots of Fire*. When I got there, I quickly realised two things. Firstly, that the kind of people who went on *University Challenge* did not spend all their time in the union bar and secondly, that very few people ran round the quads at Glasgow University.

For the first two years at university I studied lots of

subjects as was required. Tax law, corporate law, historical introduction to Scots law, or 'och aye that's how we got here' as I called it. In my third year we had to choose what subject to specialise in, and I decided to study constitutional and administrative law. You might not know what that is, but it's an area of law that has the unique benefit of being one of the least useful subjects to study if you actually want to be a 'coal face' lawyer. Very rarely would a high street solicitor encounter a client who wanted advice on whether their local authority was acting *Ultra Vires* (the concept of acting beyond given legal power or authority). I love the concept of *Ultra Vires*, although for some time I thought it was a brand of moisturiser. It's not the most useless subject I studied in my third year though. I also have a qualification in French law. So if any of you are involved in a road traffic accident in Paris and need advice on the *Loi Badinter* (a specific regime for victims of Road Traffic Accidents) I'm your woman.

When I started at university I knew that ahead of me was all the freedom in the world I could want, and it was terrifying. It turns out that my inability to make friends (see chapter on school days) was a slight disadvantage when it came to, well, making friends.

The good stuff was the lessening of the sense of isolation. The University of Glasgow had an LGB society (the T, I and Q were yet to be added) and for the first time I met people who were just like me. I'm glad that I was around at that time because it means I'm fortunate enough to have experienced the old and the new of lesbian politics. I met old-school dykes who hated men and the patriarchy, but also spent time with a new generation who were comfortable with their sexuality and place in the world and didn't remember the days of Greenham Common or burning bras. We used to have meetings, sat around a table in the union canteen, and all I really remember of that time is just how much corduroy lesbians wore. And how quickly I realised a waistcoat would increase my chances of getting laid.

But I still wasn't comfortable with who I was. The Crab of Hate sat on my shoulder and told me that I wouldn't fit in, I wouldn't be liked, I wouldn't be a 'nice' person the way I was. So I tried to fit in. And if there's one thing that doesn't help my depression is trying to be someone I'm not. The list of disasters from my time at university reads like the plot of a soap opera. A bad one mind, not one of the classics like *Dynasty* or *Eldorado*. I stumbled from one ill-advised encounter to another, hoping against hope that chance might make the answer to my problems fall into my lap.

The biggest disaster was going out with boys. Despite knowing I was gay, I decided that perhaps the reason I hated myself so much was because of my sexuality. Maybe, I reasoned, I was just doing it for attention and it was all part of my desire for reassurance. What better way to be noticed than to be gay in Glasgow, a city where it would be easier being a vegan in an abattoir. I became more and more convinced that if I was straight I would be happy. Then I could join in with my friends on double dates, going to the rugby, drinking warm white wine at university balls, and I wouldn't feel so odd and different. My first outing on the gay scene in Glasgow was to smoky bars in basements, hidden away from 'normal' society. It felt secretive, abnormal, a bit frightening and wrong.

So I tried. I went out with boys. Some of them for quite some time. And it was awful. Truly awful. Not because I hate men, far from it. I think you're all wee sausage sandwiches. If I found a man in my house I wouldn't hurt him, no. I'd pop a wee glass over his head, a piece of paper underneath and I'd pop him outside. But trying to be straight didn't help me, it just made me feel worse in a way. More of a failure. More of an outsider.

I did meet some smashing people, though. And for the first time in my life I made some friends, real and close relationships, some of which have lasted until the present day. But without question I got some things wrong, I pushed people to their limits of understanding and drove them away. As I said, I'd never really had anyone I felt I could talk to before and so I went a bit overboard in my four years' studying. You may have seen a David Attenborough nature programme where a starving lion jumps on a bison and feasts like it hasn't eaten in a year. Emotionally, I was exactly the same. I loved the attention that I got from admitting I had depression, and for the sheltered seventeen-year-olds I met I was exotic, interesting, dangerous. I was like a rare butterfly who would be wheeled out at parties, I explained the lyrics of Smiths songs to my cheerful peers, secure in the knowledge that they could never truly understand how it felt to be me!

In short, I was a bit of an arse. Instead of addressing the issues that made me depressed I was wallowing in the attention that I got. But I pushed it too far. I became too dependent on flatmates and friends. I used the condition as an excuse for bad behaviour and drunkenness, for not listening or remembering what was happening in others' lives. And gradually I drove some really lovely people away. I had to be the centre of attention, and I used my cutting and my sadness as a way of blackmailing people to stay my friends.

I fundamentally lacked the basic skills one might learn at school of how to interact with a group of people, so I ended up socialising with a very good friend called 'booze'. Many, many drunken nights were spent crying and hoping that things would get better. You could get a vodka and orange at the student union for 50p and I spend many an hour morose, wallowing in my own self-pity.

One thing I did avoid at university, and have always avoided, is the use of recreational drugs. A choice which has without question turned out to be a good thing. Numerous intelligent scientists and sociologists have researched the link between drugs such as cannabis and mental health problems. The Royal College of Psychiatrists state that:

- There is growing evidence that people with serious mental illness, including depression and psychosis, are more likely to use cannabis or have used it for long periods of time in the past. Regular use of the drug has appeared to double the risk of developing a psychotic episode or long-term schizophrenia. However, does cannabis cause depression and schizophrenia or do people with these disorders use it as a medication?

Over the past few years, research has strongly suggested that there is a clear link between early cannabis use and later mental health problems in those with a genetic vulnerability – and that there is a particular issue with the use of cannabis by adolescents. Whether or not the research is correct, avoiding anything which could exacerbate my mental health problems is undoubtedly a good thing.

I don't want you to think I was some form of goody two shoes all the time, of course I tried smoking hash. Perhaps I was lucky in that I recognised very quickly that any high was not worth the feeling of worthlessness and despair that followed quickly thereafter. I've never had the desire to sit and smoke my problems away or been tempted to snort cocaine in the back rooms of comedy clubs to give me a boost of confidence. In my experience, cocaine makes those who take it unbearably arrogant and if there's one group of people who need no help in being unbearably arrogant, it's comedians.

I'm making it all sound awful and it wasn't. My time at university gave me the freedom that I craved, and I enjoyed it. I loved studying law, and the application of theory to cases is something I miss to this day. I finally got a girlfriend and found acceptance from smashing people who didn't even think that my sexuality was an issue. I graduated with an honours law degree, something I'm tremendously proud of, and set out into the world of work. Which is where I encountered a problem I'd been ignoring for the previous four years.

I mentioned at the start of this chapter that I ended up being a lawyer because it seemed like a good idea at the time. The problem is that, if you study law, at some point you have to actually start being a lawyer. And if you're someone who entered the profession because there was nothing else you wanted to do, it's fair to say you might end up slightly stumped as to what a lawyer actually does.

I suspect there are some people reading this who might think that they know what happens to young lawyers when they choose their career. After graduation you simply choose what you want to be and do it. It's a matter of looking in the mirror and saying 'I think I want to be a human rights lawyer!' or 'I want to be a criminal defence lawyer' and it happens. Sadly, the reality is very much more mundane. What actually happens is that everyone in the graduating year desperately applies for the few jobs available, no matter what type of law it means that they will end up practising. And I followed the accepted route and threw my hat into the ring of every law firm that was taking applications. After a few interviews I was offered a position in a corporate law firm and accepted it, a decision that sent me down a pathway that ultimately led to my current career.

I sometimes feel I'm a disappointment to those who ask for amusing stories from my time in law. That I don't have a more hilarious after dinner speech with anecdotes of the perpetrators of crime, like *The Benny Hill Show* crossed with *The Killing*. The common perception of legal eagles is that we swish around in gowns, shouting 'you were lying then and you're lying now!' while solving all the crimes themselves. The truth is that I've never even set foot in a courtroom. I shuffled paper and organised telecoms links. Perhaps if I had been a litigator I wouldn't have become a comedian as I would have got the attention I craved from the judge and jury.

I went from the freedom of university to the gilded cage of corporate law, and I learned very quickly that to be different was not good. People would whisper when they talked about fellow employees going off with 'stress'. The very word was said loaded with inference. They may as well have said 'weak' or 'incompetent'. I started working right in the middle of the dot-com boom when the message was work hard, work late, earn lots of money. Whatever you do, don't make a fuss.

I don't think I was particularly normal in the corporate world. I certainly didn't fit in. The people I worked with were nice enough but the girls had boyfriends who played rugby and the boys had girlfriends who watched them play rugby. I was much more friendly with the support staff in the offices, who were in every way more interesting and welcoming. And so I would spend lunch hours chatting with the secretaries instead of my contemporaries, leading once again to self-imposed isolation.

Even though I felt uncomfortable talking about who I was and how I felt, the rigour with which pretence had to be upheld was stifling. From the outside I had everything that a normal person might want. I rose to the position of senior associate in a shiny firm, I had an excellent career in front of me, enough money to enjoy life and the respect that comes with having a profession. And I hated it. Because it wasn't me.

I'm fundamentally not very good at being normal and I certainly didn't fit in very well. I started to fall back into bad habits. Drinking more, hating myself more. I would cry on a Sunday night knowing that I had to go back into work on a Monday morning. The Crab of Hate took up residence on my shoulder and settled in.

What I needed was a job where not being normal was normal. What I needed was comedy.

CHAPTER 7

FUNNY CRAZY LADY: MIND YOUR LANGUAGE

My girlfriend is suffering from depression.

She phoned me the other day and said, 'I feel like jumping in front of a bus and you're not doing anything to help.'

So I sent her a timetable.

THAT'S a joke by the way. Oh no! It's not one of mine! I found it on the Internet when I googled 'jokes about depression', and to be fair it's one of the more palatable ones. They range from the silly to the exploitative to the incomprehensible. Of course, the very definition of a joke is that it should make the person being told it laugh, which most of them don't. That's not to say that they won't make some people snigger, that's why they're there.

I don't get jokes like these sent to me by text anymore. I used to know someone who, as regular as clockwork, would ping hilarious morsels over to me. Until, after the third gag of the day that made me angry, I replied and told him to dispose of my number immediately and never to speak to me again. Oddly for someone who works in comedy, I don't really like jokes as a rule. Anyone who has ever been to see one of my shows will know that I much prefer to tell a series of rambling stories that drift away at the end. I've never been one for a set up and punchline; heck why use ten words when ten thousand is much more fun?

But many of you will have heard jokes like the one at the start of this chapter on television, or at a comedy club, or told by 'the funny one' at work, and there's no question that the subject of mental health and humour is a tricksy one. There are commentators who believe that it's such a serious topic that no one should make fun of it, and then there are those who consider that absolutely nothing should be off limits and the more the people talk about it, even as a result of an offensive joke, the better. The truth is, to a certain extent, somewhere in between, and without question attitudes to humour are inextricably linked to language, context and the general portrayal of mental health in media and culture.

I'm self-employed so probably have more time than the average person to watch television or peruse the Internet all in the name of 'research' for my work. Because of that I suspect I'm more exposed than many to the zeitgeist and its view of mental health issues. In summary, it's fair to say that the way that depression is dealt with varies wildly depending on whether you're watching Jeremy Kyle or an earnest BBC Four documentary. The tack that is taken is caught up in the mission statement of the show itself. Is the aim of the television producer to empathise and explore the story of an individual or is it to exploit and titillate? Most often, it's a bit of both.

Let me start by stating my broad position regarding how depression and mental health is, and has been, portrayed. I can say, with some certainty, that without mad people Hollywood would be bereft of ideas. Take the daddy (or mummy) of all horror movies, *Psycho*. Norman Bates is the archetypal crazy person with an Oedipus complex, murderous rage, a split personality and customer service skills that would lead to some seriously bad Trip Advisor comments. As a generality most movies portray depressives as helpless victims, suicidal misfits and loners who can't cope with life, leading to poor decision-making. *About a Boy*, *It's a Wonderful Life*, *American Beauty*, *Girl Interrupted*. You never see a film about a normal depressive, who muddles along just like the rest of us without threatening to kill themselves as a plot point every five minutes. Of course, once you step into the realm of personality disorders, bipolar and substance use disorder you get into the realms of serial killers, abusers and, let's be honest, evil.

The logic is simple. People with mental health issues aren't normal, therefore they won't react in normal ways. They're so emotional that, who knows, maybe they might lash out with a knife or an axe if someone they fancy turns them down. Watching *The Others*, which (SPOILER ALERT!) I know turns out to be about ghosts but initially you think Nicole Kidman is mad, doesn't in itself have any real effect on the way that depression is viewed in society. But it's another example of the common representation of what we're like, and if that continues to be replayed again and again on television and in cinema, it ends up being the norm for script writers and studios to accept. When there are no positive portrayals of what is a common condition that doesn't send most people into a murderous tailspin, it adds to the stigma that feeds the Crab of Hate and helps it grow to a monstrous size.

This is an important part of this book, because it's where I confess that I'm not sure about how I feel about an issue. I know! It's confusing for me as well. I pride myself on knowing what I think about everything at all times, and like being able to state with absolute and complete certainty what is right and what is wrong. For example, yoghurt is good, Petits Filous is bad (it's just cheese pretending to be yoghurt). But on this one issue, because I understand both sides of the debate, I'm stumped.

On the one hand, I abhor censorship and become nervous when one person or group is in charge of deciding what can and can't be discussed. On the other hand, there are times when I cringe at the way mental health is discussed. Freedom of speech is a crucial part of our society but then it's important to consider the rights of those who are demonised by the media. The eternal question is always: 'Is the bigger picture more important than individual cases?' Take for example another joke that I found on the Internet:

> 'I've just been offered a new job as a co-pilot for Germanwings.'
> 'You must be mental.'
> 'Yes, I am.'

Horrible, but a perfect illustration of how mental health issues and extreme tragedy soon become just another joke about mad people. I don't find the joke funny for a lot of reasons. If that was sent to me via text message I would question whether or not I was really in tune with the person that sent it to me, but as someone involved in comedy I'm not sure that I want these things banned.

What I do believe is that care must be taken when discussing a sensitive issue, but not so much care that people are worried about expressing how they feel. I want everyone to feel that they can communicate their experiences without falling foul of an unwritten code which dictates what is acceptable and what is not. Depression doesn't just strike those who are blessed with an ability to articulate how they feel, and we shouldn't necessarily judge those who are deemed to use inappropriate language as insensitive or dismiss them as not worthy of an opinion. As with many difficult issues, such as gender and sexuality, the context in which words are used is crucial, as is intention, and knowledge about the person who is being addressed.

As a comedian I am absolutely aware that language can be used for good and for evil. As a comedian I am also aware that social media means that whatever you say can be reviewed, criticised and dissected by hundreds of thousands of people. It's sometimes easy to forget that an off-the-cuff comment made on a light-hearted panel show can reach millions of people, and that editing can sometimes remove the context in which a word or phrase was used.

The stigma that is created by lazy use of prejudicial phrases is part of the current problem surrounding mental health. Words and phrases like:

Crazy
Mental
Off my head
Bonkers
Demented
Psychotic
Bananas
Batty
Cuckoo
Loony
Lunatic
Raving
Unstable
Retarded

There are many more, of course, each and every one loaded with innuendo and judgement. And most of us will have been called one of the above or heard someone else described in such a pejorative way and shuddered internally. Some of the phrases are simply insulting, but some create a more insidious and dangerous environment, one of victimhood.

Take the most basic of phrases, and one which I myself have used in this book. 'MENTAL HEALTH ISSUES'. It's terrifying. It may as well be accompanied by screeching violins and a title sequence by Saul Bass. 'THIS WOMAN

HAS MENTAL HEALTH ISSUES! LOCK UP YOUR CHILDREN!' I'm often sent questionnaires by journalists to fill in and most of them have the stock question: 'What's it like having mental health issues?' It's a label and one that comes loaded with incredible prejudice and fear.

Comedy is as guilty as the next profession when it comes to lazy language for a cheap laugh. 'I went mental this weekend!' proclaims a stand-up to a cheering audience who equate 'going mental' to have too many beers and vomiting on themselves in a taxi. I myself was pulled up on social media once for saying I went 'insane' about something, and I'll be honest it made me hugely angry. I was incensed that someone was attempting to censor me in what I wanted to say.

There's a fine line between correctly attempting to change the way that language around mental health is used and becoming a pious mob publicly shaming people for their inappropriate use of loaded terminology. Let's face it, some people don't know, or worse, don't care, how such descriptions can damage or wound those people working with or living with depression. Headlines in the newspapers about celebs who've admitted they've had treatment being labelled as mad or bonkers, can in a very real way stop the average Joe from admitting they have a problem.

I talk about my depression frequently in my act and I'm proud to do so. Just because my head makes me feel sad doesn't mean that the only artistic expression for it is through poetry or interpretive dance for goodness sakes.

Joking about suicide may be incredibly uncomfortable for some, but it's cathartic for others and, more than that, can be bloody funny. In my opinion, the way to try to break a stigma is to smash it down, even by using language that offends to get a deliberate reaction. For example, I could say that, in the past, I was a self-harmer or I could explain that I was a cutter. Self-harming is a more polite way of referring to it, it's almost Victorian in its way of expressing what happens. Because to say you self-harm doesn't reveal what actually happens, the audience can gloss over it secure in the knowledge that I probably meant that I just slapped myself on the face sharply as a reprimand. To say I'm a 'cutter' is blunt, in your face, and cannot be misconstrued as anything other than what it is. Deliberately cutting yourself until you bleed. It's uncomfortable, and quite rightly so. It's a way of making those listening almost feel what I feel about my past.

But that to me is the brilliance of language, of what we can do with it. I may talk about my depression and be deliberately offensive so that I get people talking when they leave my shows. Because I want people to understand how important it is to talk about it. Context is incredibly important in these situations. You have to feel your audience (not literally) and probe them (again not literally) to find out where their limits are and how far you can push them. The best comedians are adept at this push me/pull you dance with punters. At starting off gently and ramping up the tension to achieve their desired conclusion.

I've spent a great deal of time trying to work out if there's a better way of using language to describe what I and millions of other people have, but it's difficult. What you need is a broad description, like 'mental health issues', which indicates that it's a genuine medical condition but which breaks free of past preconceptions that the general public have about it. Perhaps we could call it 'brain sadness pain' or 'vacillating head malaise'. It won't work though. Changing the name of something takes decades, for goodness sakes. I still call a Snickers bar a Marathon.

Should we challenge people who use 'mental' to describe something that's just a bit out of the ordinary? Yes. But perhaps no. It takes an enormous amount of confidence to stop someone mid-sentence to tell them that what they're saying is offensive to you. I'm as guilty as anyone for letting these things go, partly because of previous experience. There was a fashion for a while, and it still goes on, for people to describe something rubbish or girly as 'gay'. I'd hear people saying 'that's so gay' meaning that it was a bit silly or stupid. I confronted a comedian backstage once about his use of the term in his act and he was utterly and completely devastated. We had a huge discussion about it and I explained that it was continuing society's attitude to people like me and I thought he was going to give up comedy there and then.

For the second time in this book, I'm going to admit that I don't know the answer to this. Should I be the language police? Is it up to me to make sure that depression is treated appropriately by absolutely everyone, everywhere? What would it achieve to make people feel terrible about themselves? Despite many experiences in life, I still fundamentally believe that the majority of human beings are excellent people who don't use terminology in a malicious way.

An undoubted consequence of any attempt to censor will be the traditional cry of 'it's political correctness gone mad!' The *Daily Mail* will have headlines about 'lunatics taking over the asylum' and it could do more harm than good in the long run.

Fundamentally, I don't believe in censorship. I don't like people tweeting others with pious rebukes about the way that they've characterised their own or other people's behaviour. I cannot make the world behave the way that I want it to, even though I think I would be an amazing overlord to you all. I want to be able to joke about my depression on my terms. Not wondering if I've used the right terminology or if I'm taking the right line according to professional bodies or medics. It's from the heart, it's how I manage to express myself. Comedy should be funny first and foremost. If you want a scientifically correct lecture then you should probably go to a university.

I've no doubt that the language I've used in this book may be offensive to some, and there will be times that I may have described my own condition on stage in a way that could upset those listening. But this is the way that I choose to do things. The only real solution is for me to get my own show on BBC One where I can set forth my view on life and change attitudes. I'll probably call it

'SUSAN!' and have my name in neon lights behind me, like Elvis. I'll wait by the phone for their call. I suspect I'll be waiting for a while.

CHAPTER 8

SO, WHAT'S IT LIKE, THEN?

THE DAY-TO-DAY

YOU may have been reading this book thinking, 'That's all well and good Susan, but get to the nitty gritty, the juicy stuff. Tell us what it's really like to be depressed.' And believe me I understand your desire for information, although I would hope that my confessions of suicide attempts and self-harming would be sufficient to keep you happy through the first half of the book. Of course I know that that it wouldn't be a proper confessional tome without the close to the bone confession bit. And I totally get it. I consider myself a nice human being but I'm happy to admit that I like a bit of proper emotional gossip to chew over. I've had a sneaky look at low-rent websites and raised an eyebrow over scurrilous rumours about celebrities and their sex lives. Not that I consider myself a celebrity, far from it. I was turned away from a glittering awards ceremony once for not being on the list of invitees, which was even more embarrassing given I was nominated for one of the awards.

Let's dispense with formalities and dive right in, shall we? I've described my periods of depression for you as honestly as I can and with minimal editing, but again I'd like to reassure readers that these periods arrive far less often than they did in my youth. You mustn't worry if you meet me, I won't start weeping on your shoulder. I might sniff a bit but that could just be allergies.

I've tried to summarise the types of darkness I experience by detailing them in individual categories and, if I'm lucky, I'll just get one type of sadness at a time. Unfortunately, if I'm having a bad run they might pile on top of me like a collapsing pyramid of cheerleaders. The main thing to know while you're reading my confession is the way that I feel during these times is, almost always, not real. The emotions are truthful at the time but more often than not they aren't based in reality. Depression has a talent of distorting the actuality of life, like looking at myself in a cracked mirror. I can always see what's right in front of me but it's damaged in some way, distorted to the extent that I'm not quite sure of what's there and whether or not it really exists.

The 'no one loves me, everybody hates me, I think I'll go and eat worms' type

Sometimes I genuinely wake up believing that there's not a single person in the world that cares for me. That nobody in the whole entire planet loves me and if I disappeared tomorrow no one would notice or give two shits. It's a bleak headspace to inhabit, and the way that I feel during those times are emotions that I wouldn't wish on my worst enemy. This supposition is easily negated and demonstrably wrong, but logic doesn't matter when the darkness descends. The trouble with being in such a fugue state is that it's difficult to be rational, to look at my wife and think that she loves me, to know that I have friends and family who would be distraught if I wasn't around. I don't blame humanity and I certainly don't believe that I'm not loved because the people in my life are horrible, it's about me. My brain tells me that there's not a single thing about me that's worth loving, no redeeming features, no talents, nothing. It sounds harsh but that's the way my mind works, there's not a single person in the world that I'm harsher on than myself.

These episodes usually end up with a pity party with only one guest. Me, sitting in my house, alone, wailing and drowning in tears. Although that's not an unusual event. One absolute truth you need to know about me is that I cry. A lot. All the time. There's not a day that goes by where I don't cry at something. In Japan they have crying hotels where you can rent a room for an hour for a good weep in your lunch hour. I think we should have one of those in every town and city in the land, if nothing else it would be somewhere for me to go when I'm on tour. I've often been told that I'm too emotional but I've always been deeply affected by what people say to me or my perceptions of what people think of me.

I know that my propensity to leak water from my eyes makes people uncomfortable, especially if it seems to come out of nowhere, and I do I try to keep it under control.

I make excuses like 'Sorry my eyes are watering because I'm trying not to sneeze' or the good old excuse 'Sorry I have cat hair in my eye'. My crying problem is exacerbated by the fact that I don't cry in a discreet way, I sob. My nose runs, my eyes swell up, and I become so dehydrated that I more often than not get a migraine and am violently sick. In short, everyone within a five-mile area knows when something has upset me.

One of the difficulties of this type of depression is managing my symptoms while attempting to carry on with life without frightening anyone. My hysterical sobbing is as terrifying a spectacle as watching *Jaws* while treading water in the middle of the ocean, and I know that it can be surprising and uncomfortable for those who experience it. I have to be careful when I'm out in the real world for fear of someone videoing me in floods of tears for no apparent reason. I often travel to London by train and have, in the not so distant past, spent the whole four-and-a-half-hour journey trying not to sob. I do this by avoiding anything that might trigger an outburst. So no songs by Fleetwood Mac, no videos on Facebook of heroic animals and absolutely no alcohol.

I don't just accept my fate though, I've spent a lot of time trying to understand my firmly held belief that I'm worthless, asking myself the question, *How much love do I need in order to feel truly loved?* Sadly, I have a feeling that the only thing that would do would be to have crowds of people chanting my name, perhaps statues erected in my likeness in the high streets across the land. Capital cities called 'Calmanville', maybe public holidays on my birthday. Essentially I need to be Kim Jong-un. Something that I'm not sure that is either possible or indeed desirable.

The 'I'll just drink through it' type

My relationship with the demon drink has fluctuated wildly through my life and I'm sure that there is an alternate universe somewhere in which I've succumbed to temptation to find solutions in the bottom of a pint glass of brandy. Thankfully, in this universe I have no real problem with alcohol, but that's partly because I'm extremely careful about how much I drink. There was a time when I was drinking too much, too early in the day, and without the element of company that can make an evening in the pub with friends a lot of fun. After a brief feeling of euphoria, alcohol simply makes any symptoms that I have worse. I become more paranoid, I am more prone to crying (if that's possible) and the day after a binge my anxiety can go through the roof. Knowing that these are undesirable side effects I've implemented some life rules to prevent disaster:

1. Never drink alone.
2. Never drink in my house.
3. Never drink to forget.

Simple enough you might think but being sober can be difficult given that my profession pretty much revolves around alcohol. During my first few years at the Edinburgh

Fringe festival I don't believe that there was a single day for the whole month that I didn't have a drink. Most of my gigs are performed in licenced premises and, certainly in my early career, I was often paid in free drink provided by the venue. Part of managing depression is admitting what sets it off and removing it from your life, even if you really, really like it. And I really, really like drinking. Some of the best nights of my life have been spent in pubs, drinking pints and solving the world's problems. But there are also the bad ones. The nights when I've used alcohol for courage and stayed up late into the night on my own, downing shots in an attempt to numb my brain.

When I embarked on my tour last year I made the decision not to drink for the duration of the time I was away from home, which totalled about eighteen months in all. Not only does alcohol slow my reactions on stage but it can add to an already difficult situation by exacerbating paranoia and loneliness, emotions that I knew would crop up on a regular basis while I was travelling. My day would generally go something like this:

- Get up, have solo breakfast in budget hotel.
- Get on a train, get on another train, get on another train.
- Arrive at destination.
- Check into budget hotel.
- Travel to venue, perform show.
- Arrive back at budget hotel at 10 p.m. Go to sleep.
- Get up, have solo breakfast in budget hotel, etc., etc.

Now, I love a budget hotel. They're generally clean, with free Wi-Fi, and without their existence I couldn't do my job. But they are soulless, full to the brim with lorry drivers and travelling salesmen, most of whom would rather be anywhere than where they are. So after a hard day of comedy I had two options open to me: a) have a drink in the bar with the other depressed people or b) have a drink in my room with one depressed person. It was a difficult decision at times not to indulge, but it was the right one. You never know when life is going to pop along and kick you in the teeth and, psychologically, it's important to be prepared.

On one such occasion, I was having breakfast in a budget hotel in the middle of February on a cold and dark day. Ahead of me was another three days of travel to places I hadn't heard of to audiences who may or may not like me. I was staring at a plate of bacon and beans when a small child approached me. She was cute as a button with a huge smile on her face, a real sweetie. I often get children approaching me because (surprisingly) I do a lot of work on kids' TV and children think I'm nice. I carefully placed my knife and fork down and smiled back. She said, with great volume, 'Didn't you used to be on television?' and walked away. I picked up my knife and fork, thanked the sensible part of me for not being hungover and congratulated myself for not having children of my own.

I haven't found the cure for my depression yet, but one thing I know for sure is that it won't be found at the bottom of a bottle. I've made the choice to be very careful about my alcohol intake because I know what it can do to me. I firmly believe that if there are areas of my life that I can control, that I can take responsibility for, then I should. And I do. I'm also quite fortunate that I have very particular tastes when it comes to drinking. I only like beer or champagne, classy chick that I am. I can't stand spirits or wine, and so I am automatically limited at times by the selection of alcohol available. There are times when people have questioned the fact that I don't drink wine specifically, for example at dinner parties or corporate functions. Before I explain that I simply don't like the taste of a Merlot I'll often be met with the panicked look of a person who thinks they've just offered an alcoholic a drink.

In summation, don't be surprised if you see me with a mineral water of an evening when everyone else is blootered. I'm just taking care of myself.

The 'paranoid and full of self-doubt' type

I need to try to keep control of my paranoia. Without question it's what's caused the destruction of many relationships with friends and partners. Joyously, I've many different types of paranoia, ranging from thinking that people are talking about me but also worrying that they *aren't* talking about me. Throughout the years I've imagined many personal slights that haven't happened, fashioned arguments in my head with people who probably don't even know that I exist and mistaken innocent looks for aggression.

Of all of the types of depression I have, this is the one

that can be the most debilitating and destructive. My distorted perceptions affect how I interact with people, when I should make judgements based on the truth of relationships. I often think that people are laughing at me, which may sound like a strange thing for a comedian to dislike but I hate it. I love people laughing with me, when I've given them permission to do so, but I can't stand it when I feel that people are laughing at me. It makes me feel like I'm a kid, standing in a circle of bullies, while they point and guffaw at my expense. Of all the things that I've worked on in my life, learning to lighten up and let people laugh at something I've done is the most difficult. I hate being made to feel stupid, but the intention of those having a giggle at my expense is rarely deliberately cruel. It's simply people having fun. Lightening up isn't easy, but it is essential to maintaining friendships.

There are times when I've actually thought I deserve to feel the way I feel. That in some strange way fate has determined that I shouldn't be happy. In lucid times I know that such thoughts are rubbish, that I'm a good person and that no one deserves to feel as bad as I do, that there isn't some predetermined course that dictates my future. But it's easy in hindsight to be rational.

Paranoia is a cruel master, and the feelings it conjures up can become a self-fulfilling prophecy. I think that person is looking at me strangely, so I'll become more defensive when I see them, which leads them to think I'm being aggressive or awful, which means that they look at me funny. In an effort to combat this particular type of depression I've become much more proactive in my relationships.

I will now email and ask people if I've done something wrong. If I have I can deal with it, if I haven't I can move on. I'm sure it can be quite strange for some of the people in my life to receive a random message asking if, four weeks last Tuesday, I did something wrong, but people are getting used to it. In another twenty years they might even find it endearing.

The 'anxious' type

In a cruel irony it's very possible to be both anxious and depressed at the same time. All the fun of lethargy combined with mounting anxiety is the Catch 22 of mental health. I've found myself crying on the sofa, huddled under bundles of blankets, looking at the state of my flat as the dishes and ironing pile up, worrying about not completing work thinking, *I'll just do it all tomorrow*. Then tomorrow comes and I still can't do it. I hate going to social events because it makes me anxious, but then feel depressed when no one asks me to their party because I've told them I hate social events.

My anxiety means that I try to take control of every possible situation so that I can cope with everyday life. But it also means that I often overreact if things don't go the way that I expect. My requirement to plan is something that my wife has learned to accept, although I know it's not easy. We were going somewhere the other day and my wife casually mentioned that she was wearing a different pair of jeans than the ones she said that she was going to wear (because I had, of course, asked her to lay everything out the night before). It's irrational, and unreasonable and awful, but I got so upset at the change that it was quite distressing. I don't try to control her, far from it. The reason I love her is that she is an intelligent, powerful woman who knows her own mind. But for some reason I feel comforted and calm if I know exactly what my environment is like.

My mind is always at the highest DEFCON level possible, but the truth is that I can't control everything. I wish I could. Instead, I meticulously plan and worry and imagine the worst case scenarios for everything. I have multiple weather apps on my phone, ten different travel information sites bookmarked and a wind-up radio and torch in my emergency drawer in case the zombie apocalypse finally happens. Why do I have hundreds of toilet rolls in my cupboard? Because when society collapses that (and water) will be the most valuable commodity for bartering. I really need to relax more.

The 'press self-destruct' type

In the next room of my mind palace is the most dangerous type of depression, and it's hidden behind a door that should have a sign on it saying 'Warning. Danger of Death'. There are times when I've been so down that I've actively self-combusted. I've been as low as I think it's possible to be, I've done the self-harming thing (although I haven't done so in decades) and as you know now I even tried to kill myself. I just couldn't stand who I was or what my life was and genuinely didn't know what else to do. I should have talked to someone, of course. And whenever people ask me why I am so open about how I feel and about my life, I know it's because of that one time in my life when I felt completely alone. I can't sit with you in your house and hold your hand but I can tell you that you are not alone. There are people who can pull you out of the hole that you find yourself in. Find them.

The self-pity and jealous type

Facebook is brilliant for this one. Hours of fun scrolling through friends and exes, spitting rage at their achievements. *Why did they get that? Why wasn't I asked? How dare they have such a happy life?* It's the least attractive trait in the world to be jealous of others. To sit mired in your own self-pity, raging at unfairness of the world. Shaking my fist at the sky, wailing at the moon and shuddering at the thought of the success of others.

This type of depression is all about excuses. 'I didn't get that job because I'm Scottish/a woman/gay/short/brunette/fat.' The mind makes comparisons (as we all do), but depression helps ramps it up to the max and compiles intricate conspiracy theories to explain them away. Inevitably it leads to anger. Fizzing, festering anger at the pit of my stomach, filled with impotent rage at unnamed producers and commissioners.

It's terribly unattractive and absolutely counterproductive in every single way. Whining and moaning about everyone apart from me absolves me of responsibility for my own life and for the choices that I make that pilot my own destiny. As Albus Dumbledore so wisely said, 'It is our choices, Harry, that show what we truly are, far more than our abilities.' Refusing to accept that I have control over my own life is to allow the Crab of Hate a victory that it doesn't deserve. But it often takes incredible emotional strength to admit that the choice I make, when I retreat into a cave of self-pity, is the worst one I could possibly make.

So there you have it. That's me and my depression. I sound like a lot of fun, don't I? What do you mean, no?

I'm off to cry in a Japanese hotel room for a while.

CHAPTER 9
TELL ME HOW YOU'RE FEELING:
TALKING TALKING TALKING HAPPY TALK

A common theme through this book is communication. Of people talking about how they feel and making sure that their voices are heard. However, before you make a leap into the unknown and start blabbering away, it's worth making sure that the people you talk to are the right people. I know from personal experience that emptying your head to the wrong person can be as damaging as not talking at all. In many ways my life closely mirrors that of Cleopatra. I've made some terrible mistakes, trusted the wrong people and I've gone far too heavy with eyeliner.

Of course, if you'd known me when I was younger you would have said that I never stopped talking. And even in the present day it's difficult for some people to imagine that I have a verbal blockage of any kind. I can talk for Britain about almost anything, but while I jabber away about this and that, what is far more interesting is what I *don't* chat about. Not telling people how badly things are going, how I feel, when things are bothering me. And it's fair to say that one of the reasons for my reticence is the difficulty in knowing whom, outside of the medical profession, I could open my heart to. It's often difficult enough for people with mental health issues to admit to themselves that they have a problem, never mind tell someone else what's wrong with them. And you, like me, may have had bad experiences after opening up to friends who have reacted negatively, or even worse haven't reacted at all.

Before you book a holiday or buy a car, you'll probably do some research or at the very least take some time to think about what you're about to do. I've had friends who spend three weeks researching what type of trainers they should buy before spending another month writing endless lists of pros and cons. Take the same amount of time that you might when changing your brand of shampoo or picking a restaurant, considering a few questions about the person you're about to confide in:

1. *Do you trust the person?* Do you have a gut feeling that they will keep your confidence?

2. *Are they in a position to deal with your problems?* Are they having a tough time that might mean they don't have the reaction that you want?

3. *Where and how do you tell them?* You might well feel comfortable chatting to someone over a cup of tea in a break room, but they might not.

4. Do you think that you will continue to see this person after you've revealed your problems? Will they become part of a mutual support system that will continue for some time?

If the responses are mostly encouraging then you might well be on the right track. If not, then perhaps hold off for a bit. Maybe even test them out with a question that won't make you cry, like 'this weather makes me feel a bit down'. If they respond with a robust 'pull yourself together you weak idiot' then you're right to be concerned.

I often find it's useful, prior to judging how well a friend deals with your admission that you have depression, to think about how well you would react in a similar situation. What would you do if faced with someone confessing an emotional problem?

How many times have you asked someone 'How are you?' and before the person you're speaking to responds you say, 'I'm fine thanks.' So the whole thing runs: 'How are you, yeah I'm fine thanks.' There's a fundamental conversational discord happening between asking a question and actually listening to the answer. Of course, sometimes people don't really want to know the answer. I can't tell you how many times I've watched friends trapped by an emotional torrent after a casual and well meaning 'How are you?' And a conversation about feelings is the most terrifying place to be trapped because there's no easy way out. Usually in a dull or awkward chat you would wait for an appropriate moment to make your excuses and leave. But when someone's pouring their heart out, is there ever really an appropriate time to withdraw from the conversation? 'So it was then that I found out he was cheating on me with my best friend.' 'Really, wow, that's awful. Oh look, chipolatas!'

I don't think people should ask the question 'How are you?' unless they are fully prepared for the answer and fully prepared for it no matter how awkward it is. If you aren't ready to accept the worst-case scenario, why not ask a completely neutral and non-emotional question like, 'What's your favourite type of penguin?' Unless the person you're speaking to has had an unfortunate incident with a penguin, this will set the scene for a conversation almost entirely devoid of emotion. And, in my experience, I only encounter someone who's had an incident with a penguin, on average, one time in twenty.

I bottled everything up for years until, in my late teens, I realised that I was boring myself with my constant self-loathing. Like the person in your office that talks about how wonderful their children are constantly and without any suggestion of respite, until you wish you could shut them up using the force of your own mind? That was me, about myself.

Eventually I did start talking and some friends didn't take it very well. To be fair, in some ways I have sympathy for those who've run a mile from me. If a mate of yours who appears to be happy, healthy and normal suddenly says, 'Actually I'm falling apart' it can be frightening. The media has a history of portraying people with mental health issues as absolute fruitcakes who can be a danger to themselves and others. A friend saying they've got depression is like finding a puppy left on your doorstep. You have no idea how much work it's going to take but you have a feeling you might end up cleaning up a lot of shit.

Prepare yourself by trying to evaluate the level of emotion the person you're talking to can take by considering the very basic question: 'How much is too much?' Deciding exactly how many truth bombs to lob is a delicate balance and depends on a number of factors. Firstly, how well do you know the person that you're speaking to? If you're chatting to a very dear friend then you can express more than you would if you're, for example, talking to a stranger at the bus stop or enquiring about a direct debit at the bank. Gender does make a difference. Many men are extremely good at listening and providing advice but watch out for the warning signs. If the gent that you're talking to starts to look as if they might gnaw off their own hands to get away, perhaps scale back the emotion. Similarly, if you're speaking to a woman be careful of passive aggressive comments like 'Of course, not everyone's as strong as me when it comes to coping' or 'Do you think that the fact you're overly emotional is the reason you're not good at holding down relationships?'

And what happens after you empty your head? What do you want the person on the receiving end of such a lovely present to do? Occasionally, friends would be proactive with me and make suggestions about how to make myself feel better. It's always a joy when someone does that when you're depressed, nothing makes me smile more than someone saying: 'You know what would cheer you up!' And through the years I've tried some of the ideas just so my friends think I'm making an effort. In no particular order, here are some of the things that have been suggested to me to cheer me up that most definitely *haven't*:

1. *Expressing myself through the medium of dance.* I can't dance, so all I really expressed was the fact that I hated the fact I couldn't dance. Also, I don't know if you've ever tried to throw the shape of the emotion caused by someone writing something offensive about the way you look on an Internet forum, but it's not easy.

2. *Expressing myself through music.* Well, I say that. It was just karaoke really and after a few drinks the only song that counts to a depressed person is 'I Will Survive' which, depending on which end of the depressed spectrum you are at, is either a victory song or a promise to your family.

3. *Expressing myself through poetry.* It's something that was suggested to me as a more appropriate way of making my thoughts real. Except I've always found poetry a little bit difficult and I've always been an actions rather than words kind of girl. I'd prefer someone remembers what I take in my coffee rather than write me a sonnet. But it seemed like a good thing to do, and many of the most famous poets were all brooding and difficult. And so I sat down to write. It didn't go well, and instead of reams of poetry describing what I was going through I had a page of words that could've been written by a three-year-old. Looking at my writing, I realised that I would never be a poet, and I felt worse than when I started.

4. *Eating healthily.* There are lots and lots of studies that indicate what we eat has a great effect on our mental health. So eating well can increase one's feeling of well-being. The problem is that, by its very nature, it involves eating a lot of salads and vegetables. I've always viewed such food as an accompaniment to a main meal, like a curry. So the prospect of having a salad for a main meal unnerves me. Sometimes my wife asks if I want soup for dinner and I have to explain that soup is not a meal. Soup is what you have before a meal, or indeed it can be served in a mug and therefore drunk with a meal. It is not in itself a meal. It barely amuses my bouche. On the days that I have been at my lowest I can honestly say that a radish has never made me feel better.

Fundamentally, it's not fair for us depressives to tell our innermost secrets to a friend and not expect them to react. If you want neutrality then you may as well talk to a wall. And I wouldn't recommend that, unless you have particularly understanding wallpaper. Prepare yourself for the fact that people will give you advice on your depression whether you want it or not, and in the same way as you should be cautious in who you tell, you should also be vigilant as to the nature of the advice you may be given.

In addition, I know it sounds hypocritical in the middle of a book about depression to tell you not to listen to people who write about depression, but deciding what the intention behind the information is and from what perspective the person writing any articles is coming from is crucial. Who is giving the advice? Why are they giving it? And where are you finding it? I have always been wary of any information that may be gleaned from any of the following resources:

1. *Women's magazines.* It's quite fashionable these days to bash women's magazines for what they stand for and I don't want to take shots at an easy target, but they are a tricky place to find help. It's tough for me to read an article on how to become more self-confident only a couple of pages after the publication had exposed celebrities for having cellulite. There are pockets of joy that have tried to take a different tack (for example, the online magazine *Standard Issue* which definitely does treat mental health properly), but generally they simplify concepts in order to say the same things but with different pictures.

One of the most common ways that traditional glossy mags talk about traumatic incidents is to talk about 'closure'. What does closure even mean? It's a term that most people don't understand but everyone seems to want. When did we change from 'don't make a scene' to 'I want closure'? It, of course, means that you're over something, which is in direct contradiction to perhaps the most fabulous of all the traits of the British. The slow burning, unexpressed emotion. It's what we're famous for. In literature our great heroes are people who have no ability to say what they actually think. Mr Rochester was, I think it's fair to say, rather stand-offish. You wouldn't want to go caravanning with Professor Snape. And Miss Havisham sat in her house, in her wedding dress, and did she say anything? No. Humiliated and heartbroken, she remained alone in her decaying mansion – never removing her wedding dress and wearing only one shoe, leaving her wedding cake uneaten on the table. But more than that, she trained her adopted daughter to break men's hearts the way that hers was broken! That's genius! She doesn't want the pain to end. She doesn't want closure. She wants it to keep going. And she wants to use the next generation as well! She's done the ultimate British thing – she has infected other people with her own depression!

2. *Television stars*, particularly people who have appeared on reality TV shows. I'm sure they are nice people but they often seem to me to have a very definite agenda. Let's be honest, a failed suicide or some self-harming can get you on the front page of the tabloids. I would never dismiss anyone's story of depression, but I would be careful to consider how much of it has been filtered through the eyes of the red tops.

3. *Twitter* is a hotbed of solutions and trite sayings to help you through the bad times, but there is no way in the world that mental health problems can be solved in 140 characters. Slogans and motivational quotes can be useful for a confidence boost occasionally, but they are most certainly not a solution.

4. Bloggers. The Internet has provided a voice for many, many different voices, many of which have lots of very useful things to add to the debate on the treatment of depression. Some of them don't. Some of them will post beliefs or suggestions that will be very bad for you.

Try to remember that your thoughts are incredibly valuable, so make sure you don't blurt them out to someone who won't take care of them. Imagine you're telling someone the location of the Ark of the Covenant – would you trust them not to tell the bad guys? Would they help you on your quest to recover it? In other words, just think 'What would Indiana Jones do?' and you'll be fine.

CHAPTER 10

I CAN'T GO TO A SHRINK, I'M BIG ENOUGH ALREADY! SHRINK SHOPPING

ONE important topic I've conspicuously avoided so far is the matter of psychiatry, therapy and psychologists. The professionals when it comes to dealing with my sort. And there's a good reason for my reticence, it's because (and don't get upset with me immediately) I truly believe that sometimes therapy doesn't work. Not because the method is incorrect or that it's a bad thing to do, but because it's really, really easy to talk to the wrong kind of therapist. I've personally had some horrific experiences when I've sought help, which put me off doing anything about depression for some time after the event. Often people don't share these stories because to do so is to admit that you sought help in the first place and also because there is a certain sense of failure that falls heavily on your shoulders when something that's meant to help doesn't.

If you input a quick Internet search for 'depression and treatment' you'll find numerous pages with lots of different types of counsellors and therapists, each offering a way of helping. I've spent a great deal of time researching the difference between psychiatrists, clinical psychologists, psychotherapy and counsellors (honestly, the cold winter nights fly by in my house) and I'm sure you can have a fun afternoon doing the same. The fact that there are so many ways to seek help is a wonderful development, but the fact that there are so many treatments available can also be incredibly intimidating when trying to choose the right one for you.

Let's start with some basics because when it comes to therapy there are numerous exciting sounding ways to spill your soul. The most common talking therapies offered on the NHS are psychotherapy, cognitive behavioural therapy (CBT), counselling, family therapy, couples therapy and group therapy. Each have their own distinctive role and some may suit needs better than others.

Alternative therapies often work well for people with anxiety and depression, and I've also had a fairly successful track record when I've broken out of my comfort zone of conventional treatment. I've used acupuncture to eradicate the migraines that often accompany my general feeling of malaise. It's a slightly strange feeling to pay someone to stick pins in your head, but once you get over the fact that you look like a character in a horror movie it feels rather relaxing.

More recently I used hypnosis to try to calm the anxiety that I feel when I have to fly. As I mentioned earlier, I take Diazepam when I have to travel, but I realised that it would become awkward to drug myself when travelling solo. I decided to see if I could find a more natural way to control my feelings, and part of me was hopeful that it might also assist my general feelings of tension and worry. It's important to know how difficult this task was. I wasn't just a bit upset about getting on a plane. For years the very act of getting to a foreign place was as difficult as getting more than one woman on *Mock the Week*. I was once removed from a plane for screaming 'we're all going to die'. I would be physically sick at the mere thought of going to an airport, and I would sob uncontrollably if my agent offered me work that involved a flight abroad. It was my wife who eventually convinced me to go to hypnotherapy, mainly because she refused to accept that a city break in Leeds was as much fun as a fortnight in a villa in Portugal. Her exact words were: 'I'm going to leave you unless we go on holiday somewhere where the temperature is above fifteen degrees.'

I'm not a hippy or anything. Even though I approached the treatment with an open mind, I firmly believed it wouldn't work on me, that I'd be fully awake and more importantly be proven correct that it was a load of nonsense. I lay on the sofa while my hypnotherapist, whom I will refer to as Mr Magic, told me what would happen. We had spent some time prior to the treatment discussing precisely what my issues were (I thought the plane would crash), why I was worried (because the plane would crash) and what form my anxiety took (panic attacks because the plane would crash). After what must have been a tortuous consultation for Mr Magic, he came up with a plan to speak to my subconscious about my stress levels. The first step was to put me under, to hypnotise me. You might be like me – you have watched TV shows or stage shows where idiots end up dancing like chickens or taking their clothes off when someone says the key word and thought, *That would never be me, I'm far too mentally strong to be manipulated like that.*

Five seconds. That's how long it took for me to go under. My wife was in the room and was timing it. I suspect she was watching for tips on how to shut me up. I was hypnotised for forty-five minutes during which, and there's no other way to describe it, Mr Magic had a damn good rummage around in my subconscious.

We developed a series of techniques to help me when it feels like it's all getting too much. For example, we created a safe room in my mind that I can go to when I'm scared. He told me to create somewhere that had everything that makes me feel good in it, and I did, and I can see it now. A large circular room, filled with books, a log fire and a comfortable sofa on which I lie while I'm covered in cats. We programmed in a way of accessing it, by pressing together my thumb and middle finger of my right hand and closing my eyes, somewhere to hide when it all gets too much.

After some more probing, what he discovered, on a fundamental level, is that my mind has become a sort of booby trap for fun. We all have a subconscious that controls our reaction to fear of the unknown, commonly known as the fight or flight reflex. The problem is that my subconscious has gone rogue and screams 'Run!' at the thought of anything frightening. On its own, hypnotherapy was certainly not a miracle cure, but as part of a concerted effort to improve my mental health, it was a vital part of my recovery.

*

The point of this book is to be honest with you, dear reader, and that means revealing the negative experiences as well as the positive. And I'm sure I'm not alone in having bad experiences with therapists; sometimes I may have been at fault, and at times my counsellor undoubtedly was. I've noted below the warts-and-all encounters I've had over the years. I can laugh at them now, at the time I most certainly didn't. Please don't give up on treatment; it could simply be that you need to metaphorically kiss a few more frogs before you find your mental health prince or princess.

My first experience attempting a talking therapy wasn't good. I was in my teens, and I'd been sent against my will to talk to a nice lady about my weirdness. The very first time you go to a therapist is fairly terrifying, because you just don't know what's going to happen. It was like a bizarre blind date that I was paying to go on. The consultation room was bare, with lots of pine furniture from MFI and a plastic cactus upon which the dust sparkled like frost. The room smelled of Shake n' Vac and despair. I don't know quite what I was expecting but the first thing that my appointed therapist asked was, 'How do you feel?' And I clammed up. *How dare she ask me such a personal question when it was clear I was struggling with communication issues! Imagine just asking that straight off the bat! How do I feel? If it were that easy to explain I would have told someone a long time ago.* I sat, brooding and silent. So she suggested we try a different technique. She suggested I *draw* how I was feeling.

I looked at her for a sign that this was a joke. She

reiterated that I should draw my emotions. Now, there are three things that I know. Firstly, I can't draw, my artistic ability is limited to drawing a cat sitting beside a duck. Don't ask me why I can draw that, it's just something I can do. Secondly, I hate being patronised. Now I know I was young, and incidentally still look young as I continue to get asked for ID when buying alcohol at the age of forty-one, but I'm not stupid. And lastly, I'd read every book going about psychology. It's annoying I know. It must be how doctors feel knowing that every single person that they see has already diagnosed themselves via the Internet. So I knew what she was doing and she was doing it wrong.

She was insistent, however, and maintained what can only be described as a frightening level of eye contact. So I started drawing. I drew the only thing I could. A cat sitting beside a duck. She was beside herself with joy when she saw it. It represented, she said, my alienation from society. I was the duck and the world was the cat. I wanted to be a cat but I was a duck. What I needed to do was be more of a cat and then I'd fit in. I left and never went back. I'm not a duck. I resolved never to speak to anyone ever again about how I was feeling.

My second experience was similarly horrific. As you'll know from a previous chapter, I was hospitalised in my teens and I was assigned a young therapist to deal with my case. Those in charge of the ward had clearly decided that the 'youth' would react better if their therapist were a younger person, perhaps they were hoping we'd talk about rap music or graffiti art. Which doesn't work in practice. I don't care if I'm talking to an eighteen-year-old or an eighty-year-old, I just don't want them to insult me. I arrived for my outpatients' appointment in civvies, as I didn't want to wear my school uniform to the clinic. If I recall correctly, I was wearing a leather biker jacket I'd borrowed from a boy I was kind of seeing, which was a very different look for me. I suspect I'd been watching a lot of Marlon Brando at the time, and was attracted to the idea of being a leather-clad rebel. Being utterly useless in the fashion stakes, thus having limited accessory options, I paired it with a tapestry handbag that was kicking around the house and off I went. As soon as I walked in the lady therapist burst into peals of laughter and informed me, in no uncertain terms, that you couldn't have a handbag with a biker jacket and that I looked silly. What a way to start a session. Nothing says, 'trust me' quite like laughing at someone with self-confidence issues. I saw her for the required number of sessions, said all the right things, and never saw her again.

I carried on into my twenties determined not to try talking therapies again, the last two incidents had been so awful that I figured it was better just to live in misery. And so that's the way I stayed, replaying conversations over and over in my head. It was easier that way. I was a bundle of nerves and neuroses. The Crab of Hate became a constant passenger. I tried to talk occasionally but soon realised it was a useless endeavour. No one would understand me. I embraced it. I was a maverick; I was a philosopher, a writer. I was an idiot.

I made one more attempt at seeking help in my

mid-twenties when I found an advert for person-centred therapy at a clinic near my work. This was the cherry on the top of the cake of hell that my previous experiences had been. The nightmare scenario that you never want to encounter. I went for a few weeks and it was kind of going OK, I was starting to open up about how I felt and began to believe that maybe this might be the right way for me to go. Until one fateful afternoon when everything went wrong. I turned up at the appointed time and was called into the room. I sat down in my usual chair and lit a cigarette (it was still allowed in those days). I felt that my therapist seemed a bit on edge but wasn't that concerned, as Martine McCutcheon sang so beautifully, this was my moment. Very quickly the conversation took a turn for the worse.

Me: So it's just been a bit of a bad week really.

Therapist: Fine.

(Pregnant pause)

Me: Sorry, have I done something wrong? You seem annoyed.

Therapist: I'm fine.

(Nine-months pregnant pause)

Me: Are you sure?

Therapist: Actually I'm pissed off. You never ask me how I am or what's been going on with me.

Me: Sorry?

Therapist: I have feelings too you know. I really like you and you never think about me and our relationship.

(Four-weeks'-overdue pregnant pause)

Me: I think I should go now.

I left feeling guilty and strange and a bit creeped out, and so I made the same decision that I'd made every other time I'd tried therapy, never to talk to anyone else ever again and just keep my mouth shut. For the next few years I managed to function. I disguised the Crab of Hate by wearing large coats and, in the summer, shawls. Then in my early thirties things got bad again. I was filled with a new level of self-loathing and the Crab of Hate had grown to gargantuan proportions. I was spending longer and longer watching box sets and hiding on my own.

Then I decided to sort myself out. I had finally had enough of the Crab of Hate. I looked at my friends who were happy and realised that I wanted that. More than that, I was about to get married and I didn't want to start my life with my wife as a complete mess. If I didn't think enough of myself to care, I thought a lot about her and she deserved more from me. I was determined to try again with therapy.

I googled counselling services in Glasgow. There were even more to choose from than before and I began to feel the same dread that accompanied every single attempt to get help. Sadly, there's no equivalent to TripAdvisor when it comes to counselling and you simply pays your money and takes your choice. My criterion was as follows. I wanted someone young, simply because I couldn't talk to someone my mother's age about how I was feeling, because then I would be talking to my mother. But not someone too young who would criticise my dress sense or the fact I'd paired, oh I don't know, a handbag with a biker jacket. I wanted to speak to a woman, not because I don't think men are very good at counselling, I just thought a woman would better understand how I was feeling. And lastly, I wanted someone who looked like they cared. It is, in my view, an absolute truth that some people have more friendly faces than others. Think of people that you know that you would talk to and ones you wouldn't. Think of their faces, some make you want to chat; some make you want to hide your handbag.

So the criterion was simple. A woman between the ages of twenty-five and forty-five with a kind face. Which just sounds like a description on *Crimewatch*.

I found someone who fitted the bill. I made an appointment. I arrived thirty minutes early, which is awkward. If you've never sat in a crowded waiting room at a therapist's, you've missed out. Someone could walk in dressed as Princess Leia and start breakdancing and no one would look up. I've never seen such intense concentration on anything like the faces of the other people in that room in my life. No one wants anyone else to know that they're there. The embarrassment level at seeking help is astonishing. People go to the gym to work out their bodies and they can't stop telling you about it, showing you their gym kits and telling you how much progress they're making. You go to exercise your mind once a week and no one wants to know.

The only benefit is that it's a really good way of not getting people to ask specifics of what you're doing. If you say to your HR manager that you're going to the dentist they might ask, 'Oh really what's wrong?' Requiring you to tell them all about your dental issues. But if you were going to a therapist it might go: 'What are you doing today Susan?' 'Me? I'm off to a psychologist.' (Pause. Cue awkward shuffling of feet.) 'The weather's been unsettled, hasn't it?'

But I went to 'my lady', as I called her. I sat. I told her I was terrified that she would have me sectioned if I told her the truth about how I was feeling and that someone had done that before to me. She explained that unless I seemed to be a danger to others or myself she wouldn't do that. I then stated very clearly what I wasn't going to do. Absolutely no drawing of my feelings, if she wanted that I'd draw her a picture of a duck and a cat right now and stop wasting her time.

If I'm very honest, I was surprised she carried on with the appointment because all I did when I arrived was tell her what I was and wasn't going to do. But she persisted and we talked. And it was rather wonderful.

Over the course of a few months I started to embrace my feelings, I gained confidence, I learned techniques for coping and how to express myself. I can't properly express how humiliating and embarrassing and awful it was. I'd spent so long not saying anything that even expressing the simplest of emotions was a struggle. And it was a physical struggle. I would sit, wrapped in a tiny ball on the chair, stuttering and moaning as if I had a gag in my mouth or my throat was obstructed.

I would be lying to you if I said that it was easy. I hated it at times. I felt angry that someone was trying to ask me questions. I found it difficult to trust her and so fed her small bits of information at a time to see what she would do with it. I didn't tell her the truth at times, I changed my story, I was skittish and terrified. I cried a lot, I was angry a lot, and I felt sick with embarrassment. Talking therapies are not a quick fix. All the stuff that's in your head that you've been hiding or ignoring will come out at some point and when it does it can be awful. But then, with the help of the right therapist, it will get better.

I've had some terrible experiences, but then sometimes I'm not a very easy person to deal with. My life only really started working when I became determined that I wanted it to, when I started pushing through the horrific awkwardness that I felt and really talked about how I was feeling. If you do take part in talking therapies the important word is 'talking'. You have to do that bit. If it were as easy as just listening to people telling you what to do, we would all get better just from switching on Radio 4 of an evening. Being an active participant in your own recovery is crucial. Taking control of how you feel, especially at the times when you are in control and completely lucid.

Finding the right therapist can be a hellish journey, but the reward at the end can be life changing.

CHAPTER 11
THE TEARS
OF A CLOWN:
SAVED BY STAND-UP

I mentioned at the start of this book that I used to be a lawyer. And I was. Four years of work to obtain a degree, one year studying for a diploma, two years training and then seven years as a solicitor. Excitingly, I left that life of glamour behind to be a stand-up comedian, a profession that I've been proud to be a part of for the past ten years. The primary focus of my job now is to make people laugh. Sadly, a life centred around mirth doesn't mean that the life of a travelling clown is full of joy. Far from it.

Indulge me for a moment. Let's play a word association game. Clear your mind. Unless you're listening to an audiobook, in which case keep your mind on what you're doing. And if you're a doctor or something also keep your mind on the job. Actually, whatever you're doing don't clear your mind; I don't want to get sued. It's very simple, I'll give you a word and then you just think of the first thing that comes into your head. Go with your gut. First up 'Frangipane'. If you thought 'revolting' then you're correct. Next one, 'Wuthering Heights'. If you thought about Kate Bush singing and dancing then well done. If you thought of the book by Emily Brontë better luck next time, this isn't an English exam. Lastly the word 'comedian'. If you thought happy thoughts about laughter, then sorry, but you're wrong. If you thought about desolation, loneliness, narcissism and nihilism, then well done! Gold star! You've hit the nail on the head. I wouldn't be surprised if I walked into Madame Tussauds, found myself in the Chamber of Horrors and saw a specific section full of wax models of comedians headed 'where happiness went to die'. Lovely comedian Alan Davies has previously stated that he believes stand-ups can be divided into two groups, golfers and self-harmers. I guess I'm just lucky in that I'm both.

Of course, I'm generalising and being slightly rude about comedians, but I can do that, as I'm a jester by trade. I know the truth. There's no question that in many ways being a joke teller is an obvious job for me, because the common perception the public have of comedians is of a self-obsessed, drunken, depressed loner desperately seeking the affirmation of strangers. But that's not quite true. I never drink at work.

Before I started gigging myself, I expected comedy to be fun. I thought it would be a good way to be more positive about life and assumed that comedians would be joyous laughter-mongers on stage and off. The only time I've ever been more wrong was when I was younger and genuinely believed for a couple of months that Delia Smith was my mum. I was naive in the beginning of my comedy career, you see. Beside myself with excitement before my first gig, looking forward to the good-natured backstage banter, the cheerful chats betwixt the clowns, the happy camaraderie of fellow mirth makers. I was wrong. I've not made a worse mistake since I tried to woo someone I had romantic leanings towards by playing her a selection of contemporary tunes on my recorder.

Comics tend to be introspective people, constantly evaluating, observing and judging others. They have a bleak outlook, which is essential for comedy but horrific on a long car journey to Norwich. Sitting backstage at my first gigs, I listened with fear as older comics described the quest I'd have to go on to become a real comedian. It sounded like *Lord of the Rings*, crossed with *Total Wipeout* with a touch of actual torture thrown in for good measure. Misery was what made the funny. Like fertiliser on roses, if things were bad then they were good.

While I was disappointed at the lack of fun times in the green rooms of comedy clubs around the country, I also realised that it was absolutely the right place for me to be. Comedy and Calman were a perfect pairing. Like Sonny and Cher, bacon and eggs, or Nick Clegg and regret. It was the first time I'd ever encountered a group of people more miserable than I was! Maudlin? Yes. Self-absorbed? Of course! It was perfect. What other profession allows you the freedom to tell people how awful you feel, how much you hate everyone and lets you infect their joy with your misery? Well, apart from being a taxi driver.

I remember once when I was compering the Stand Comedy Club in Edinburgh; a fairly new comic was sitting nervously backstage waiting to go on. We started chatting and I started asking her the standard green room questions: how long have you been going, how many gigs have you done, are you enjoying it? I could tell that she wanted to ask me something and I eventually prised it out of her.

'I'm just so worried. I have mental health issues and I don't think I'll fit in.'

I shouldn't have laughed quite as loud as I did, but I had to break it to her that if she thought she was going to be special or different because she was depressed she needed to think again. The only thing to do is let it all out.

If I'm honest about how successful I've been, my comedy career only really started to go well when I began to acknowledge on stage how depressed I really was. In the early days I tried to write shows that contained clear ten-minute chunks of happy anecdotal material which could be easily lifted and performed on *Live at the Apollo* or *Michael McIntyre's Comedy Roadshow*. Unfortunately, that was as inappropriate a career goal as entering *Britain's Next Top Model* or aspiring to represent Scotland in the gymnastics at the next Olympics. But I only realised that I needed to change who I was on stage when I was on the verge of giving it all up.

The year was 2010, and I was performing my third solo show at the Fringe. Industry experts said that it was important for me to raise my profile and to start attracting the attention of television bookers. The problem was that the show I was performing wasn't actually that good, partly because it wasn't honest. I should say that you won't often find comedians being that honest about their own performances in Edinburgh; more often than not a comic will tell you they 'killed it' or 'blew the roof off the place' when in fact they were mediocre at best. The puff-chested performer is one of the most common sights at the Fringe and one of the least attractive. They're loud, obnoxious and feed off the blood of weaker animals.

I'm quite happy to admit that my show wasn't up to the standard it should have been, and while I performed that year to good houses, the laughter was limited and at times completely inaudible. I'm often asked in interviews to describe my worst gig, and it was without a doubt one Saturday night at the Fringe in 2010, when 150 people (a sold-out crowd) stared at me for an hour. Just stared. As a comic I know within five minutes if an audience is going to enjoy the show, and I knew that they weren't. Until you've had a large crowd of people looking at you for fifty-five minutes while you tell jokes, you haven't lived. In many ways I'd prefer an audience to hate me rather than be ambivalent. At least with anger you have an emotion to play off and to channel. When a large group of people just think 'meh', there isn't a single thing you can do about it. And even if I wanted to, I couldn't have walked off stage. At the Fringe you are contractually obliged by most venues to perform the show even if only one person buys a ticket. I've done a show to two people before. That's not so bad. As someone far wiser than me said, 'You can't die on stage if there aren't enough people in the audience to carry your coffin.'

To be fair, that's not the only bad experience I've had in my career. Just after I resigned my job as a lawyer I had my first experience of what a cruel mistress Edinburgh can be. A fellow comic said that he had secured an amazing venue for a late-night extravaganza that would become the 'must see' attraction of the Fringe. I believed him and was absolutely convinced that I would be discovered and get my own show on Channel 4 and end up in a mansion in LA within the year. It's a testament to my ignorance of the comedy scene that I genuinely had no idea just how many shows there are at the Fringe. I believe it's about 3 million (it certainly feels like that sometimes), most of which contained comedians the public had actually heard of. The run was a disaster. In total about fifteen people came to the show during the month that it was on. I tried my best to turn the situation around, but all I did was make things worse.

If you don't know Edinburgh then let me describe the place to you. In short it's Scotland's capital city, a gorgeous place blessed with extraordinary architecture and a castle. For eleven months of the year it's a busy but pleasant place to be. For one month of the year, August, it becomes the arts capital of the world and is overwhelmed by desperate artists, all of whom are fighting for the same audiences. A common way of communicating with these people is to flyer them. In basic terms that means handing a complete stranger a piece of paper with your face on it and using the three seconds you have their attention for to sell them your show. As our show was a late-night one, we had to flyer far later than I would have liked, and often took a pitch on the Royal Mile (a long busy street in the centre of town) to entice people in. It wasn't working, I had been drinking far too much cheap lager, eating far too few vegetables and more than that I was acutely aware of the fact that I was failing. All of the people who had told me I was stupid to give up my job were right, I was an idiot.

My last ditch attempt to sell the show is one of the lowest moments in my life, although it's funny in hindsight. I made myself a sandwich board out of cardboard that I found in a skip behind a supermarket. I wrote the name of the show on it and I believe it said that I would give my kidney to anyone who bought a ticket. After a few hours standing in the cold it started to rain, and my sandwich board slowly turned into papier mâché, the general public were ignoring me and suddenly, without any provocation, I was punched in the back. I wasn't assaulted by a rugby player or a ninja. No. I was punched by a small child who thought it would be funny. It was less funny for him when I chased him down the street. It worked out well though, I didn't spill a drop of my pint.

The only reason I didn't give up at that point, and I considered it, was because I didn't want all of those people who told me I was an idiot to be right. My career carried on in unremarkable style for the next couple of years until that infamous show of 2010. I was so disheartened by what I had ended up doing that I took a year away from the Fringe to take stock of what type of comic I wanted to be. It was an epiphany of sorts, and I've only ever had one similar moment in my career.

When I started off in stand-up there were certain clubs

that more experienced comics insisted were important to get in with. If you played them then you would be considered a proper comic by your peers. The Stand Comedy Clubs were one of them and I've always found them to be an excellent showcase for my profession, with caring staff and generally very receptive audiences. Many of my peers got their first real breaks in the basement of the Glasgow and Edinburgh premises and I'll be forever grateful for the help that they gave me when I was starting out.

But there was another chain of clubs that were held in high regard, less for the craft and more for the money. The standard procedure in order to get bookings was to do a series of auditions (open spots) that would lead to paid work at the weekends. I didn't particularly enjoy playing them, not because I dislike a rowdy audience, but I didn't like the 'banter' that often played between the comic and the punters. I got into this job to make people feel happier, to exercise my mind and to hopefully put across a point of view. What I didn't want to do was simply insult people. If my aim was just to be a dick I may as well get pissed and wander round the city centre on a Saturday night shouting at strangers.

My last gig for this particular chain was one of those times in life when you reach a fork in the road and you have to decide which path to travel. I was on first after the compère, who had done as good a job as possible with a dodgy sound system and the several stag nights that were in attendance. I arrived on stage to a muted response, started with my best gags, but was aware of the constant chatter at a table to the right of the stage. I broke off my set to speak to one of the gentlemen (I believe he was dressed as a penis, which was apt) and asked him what he did for a living. He said something like, 'I kill fat dykes.' A large proportion of the crowd cheered, which doesn't indicate that there's a great deal of support in the room. I was angry though and came back at him with one of my prepared put downs, one of the harshest ones I had, but stopped mid-sentence. I could have carried on insulting him and got the laughs that I needed in that way, but I didn't want to. I didn't give up my job and my career for this: to become someone who called people names for a cheap gag. So I stopped, thanked the audience, walked off stage, got into my car and drove home. I've never worked for that company again and never will. I chose the fork in the road marked 'dignity'.

There are lots of different types of stand-ups out there. Some are one-liner merchants, some are masters of puns, and some sing songs. Personally I like to see comics that make me think about things, but more than that tell me something about themselves. In my time I've seen exceptional shows by Bridget Christie, Jeremy Hardy, Tig Notaro, Michael Legge, Sarah Millican and Sue Perkins, all of them leaving me with a lasting impression of the person telling the stories.

So when I had my second epiphany, I realised that to change my style might not make me the most marketable of comedians, but it would be truthful. So I changed tack, and the first show that I wrote with this new purpose in mind was *This Lady's Not For Turning Either* which was about equal marriage and my own desire to have the right to marry. It was personal, very honest and emotional. And performing it every night at the Fringe in 2012 felt amazing. Not just in terms of comedy but in my own personal life. I finally had an outlet for all of the things that were in my head.

I was being paid to tell people how depressed I was. And I did. I was finally me! Miserable, depressed, maudlin me! And there's no question that finding comedy has been a turning point in my life. At the Fringe I get fifty-five minutes of uninterrupted time to tell people what I want to tell them. No producer or director can tell me not to. It's up to me. Last year's show *Lady Like* dealt with some of the issues of my social media problems, and while it was hard some evenings saying some of the comments out loud, it was cathartic. Without question comedy can change people's perceptions of issues. I performed around 170 gigs on my tour to maybe 40,000 people in total, and even if only ten or twenty of that number had thought about or had sent abusive messages on social media, there was a chance that after seeing the show they might understand the impact of it. Maybe they would think twice before they did it again. Of course, they might just carry on regardless, but it's worth a shot.

For someone with low self-esteem and confidence, comedy is the best and the worst job in the world. I can get on stage and, on a good night, hundreds of strangers applaud and laugh and hang on my every word. For someone who needs constant affirmation, it is truly a quick fix of love. And I know I should be cool about it and pretend it doesn't matter, but it does. If I haven't gigged in a while I start to feel jumpy and nervous and concerned about my value to society. At the end of the Edinburgh Fringe, which is thirty days of constant performance, I always have a dip in my mood. I tried to explain to my wife why it happens so she could understand why I become such a grouch when I finally drag myself home. It's difficult for her, though, she doesn't need what I need, she has enough confidence in herself without constantly being told how magnificent she is. A few years ago, in the middle of a post Fringe slump, she asked a perfectly reasonable question:

'But am I not enough for you?'

She shouldn't have asked that question because the truth is that she isn't. The bit of my soul that was missing during my teens and twenties has been filled by stand-up. And I don't mean to romanticise what it's like to perform on stage, it can be a terrible job. I've never encountered any form of entertainment that makes people quite as angry as comedy does. People can absolutely love what I do or absolutely hate it, and therefore me. Strangers have absolutely no qualms about telling me their opinion on what I've done with no consideration for my feelings, and why should they; I'm that lady off the television. Some people have said to me that I probably don't even write my own material, that I probably have a staff full of joke writers. I don't. No one else could write jokes about cats the way that I do.

Honesty from an audience is part of the territory. I

remember the first time I was on *Have I Got News For You*, which was without question a career milestone for me. I'd watched the show for years and so to actually appear on it was hugely exciting. I avoided the transmission (as I always do) and the next day went for a pint in my local pub. Now my local pub is truly my favourite place on the planet. There's no food, there's no music, there's no fun allowed at any time. You can always get a seat on a Friday night and a wonderful woman called Jo (who is the most terrifying and brilliant human being I've ever met) runs it. I've been going to the same pub now for fourteen years, and the old guys who drink there first knew me when I was a lawyer and have watched my career change with disinterest and suspicion for the past decade. The night after that first *HIGNFY* show I walked in a little nervous about their reaction. I shouldn't have worried. As I sat down one of the old men was sent across to deliver the verdict of the pub. He looked me straight in the eye and in a broad Glaswegian accent he said:

'Saw you on that show the other night. You weren't as shite as I thought you might be.'

Believe me, that's the equivalent of a five-star review at the Fringe. That quote should've gone on my posters.

Despite the clear ups and downs, I am absolutely sure that I have the perfect job. I would never encourage other depressives to jump into the pool of comedy without knowing the reality of hell that they're about to swim in, and there are simpler ways of getting better. But it worked for me. I now have a voice when I feel no one will listen, and I have a stage when I think I'm invisible. It's not an exaggeration to say that stand-up saved my life, because it did. And it continues to do so every single night.

CHAPTER 12

MODERN LIFE IS AWFUL: TWITTER FUN

CERTAIN aspects of life today can present particular challenges for the overtly maudlin among us. While the Internet ensures that there is an endless supply of box sets and documentaries to keep us company in the wee small hours, it's also a Pandora's box of worms. And if that's not an exciting mixed metaphor, I don't know what is.

I'm part of a transitional generation in that I remember what it was like before all this happened, but I've also embraced new technology with fervour. From MySpace onwards I've been online and experienced the problems and the perks of the social media age. It's a tricky world that can be incredibly difficult to negotiate, and at times real world encounters are easier to deal with than anonymous late-night forays into the world of cyberspace. I've tried to detail below my own experiences and thoughts; you may disagree with them and if you do please tweet me using the hashtag #SusanIsAwesome. Thanks.

Back in the day when I was a lad, we didn't have mobile

phones or laptops. We had landlines and any bullying happened the old-fashioned way. Usually to your face, usually in the playground and probably taking the form of some name-calling and a bit of pushing and shoving. The thing about that kind of bullying, horrific though it is and was, is that it's a very different type of pressure from the kind that you can encounter online. In the old days at least the person making you feel like crap had to actually step up and say what they were thinking without hiding behind a pseudonym or funny avatar. No one could post humiliating pictures of me online, hell, no one would take them as it cost too much money to buy the film and then have it developed. Of course, the isolation that I felt as a child was bad, but there was an end to it, I left school and left those people who made me miserable behind. Social media means that it's far more difficult to escape. Having been through both types of nastiness, there's no question that in my experience Twitter and Facebook can be far more frightening than any playground encounter that I've had. I've developed a far thicker skin over the years that I've been online, particularly with Twitter, but the first time I got a cruel tweet took my breath away.

The most common term used in the current online world is 'troll', a catch-all definition that commentators use to describe everything from someone who disagrees with your opinions to systematic abuse on a consistent basis. I always feel that to call someone a troll doesn't do justice to the kind of behaviour exhibited by some. To give someone such an innocuous name that covers such a range of behaviours almost normalises what they do. People talk about 'trolling' celebrities like it's a fun thing to do, like it's something that we should shrug our shoulders at and move on. A troll to me is the most insidious and weak of all of the bullies I'll ever encounter in my life. Whatever the reason for their crusade of misery, they will never win. If I can survive the Crab of Hate, I can survive them.

People who suggest that it's easy to ignore social media abuse or trolling fail to understand how personal it can feel. My laptop is my world in many ways. I'm self-employed so rely on the Internet for company during the day, and often on long weekends working away from home. When a particularly aggressive tweet arrives it can feel as violating as if someone had broken into my house and shouted it in my face. Many people seem to think that appearances on Radio 4 lead to rivers of gold, but it doesn't. I don't have a vast staff at my disposal that take control of my social media output. It's me, with a cup of coffee, opening my laptop at the start of the day. I like to do that because then I can interact with the many, many lovely people that do constitute the majority of followers I have.

There are some complete idiots online, stupid people who just tweet how ugly celebs are, but Internet bullies are usually very bright and they seem to have vast amounts of time to spend prodding people for fun. The key to a good troll (if I can put it that way) is identifying what makes a target the most upset and relentlessly pursuing it. For most women the way that we look can be an easy weak spot. And I've had tweets in the past regarding the way that I look which have hurt me. Some choice examples are:

I was on *Have I Got News For You* and someone tweeted me, '*Don't take this the wrong way Susan*' because there's always a right way to take a tweet that starts 'Don't take this the wrong way', '*Don't take this the wrong way Susan, but if you lost three stone you might be attractive.*' I was on the television once and someone tweeted me '*Why's this fat dyke taking up half of my television screen.*' One of my favourite comments on Facebook was '*The funniest thing about Susan Calman is the fact that she has a wife.*'

It would be easy to drive myself to madness trying to analyse some of these comments and I will admit to being shocked and rather obsessed with them when I started out in comedy. It was such a surprise you see, not that there are people in the world who are arseholes, just the sheer nastiness of the situation. I don't know if they think I haven't noticed the fact that I'm not a tiny thin person. Maybe they think that they're in some way helping me. Maybe it's a genuine attempt to be nice.

Or maybe it's my worst fear realised. That there are some horrible nasty people in the world who delight in making other people unhappy. Oddly enough, once you accept that as a possibility, things become much easier, because you can apply real-life tactics to the online world to protect yourself. If you were at a party and there was an obviously aggressive dickhead there, would you try to engage them? Would you earnestly try to explain why they were wrong or would you instead spend your time with people who don't make you feel like shit?

You may have already worked out that I'm one of those

feminists that you might have read about in the *Guardian* and I'm going to make a statement that you might disagree with now (remember, tweet your opinions using the hashtag #SusanIsAwesome). Women have it harder on social media. There, I said it. Not just in terms of how we look, although that's certainly the case. I asked my friends who are in the media, 'Who has received negative tweets about the way that you look?' All of the women, without exception, had. None of the men had. But more than that, women are routinely shut down when they have an opinion. The sheer force and volume of a trolling campaign if you happen to comment on women on banknotes, or passports or sexual health can shut down opinion. It can make people think twice about commenting. Even if you are being attacked, it's very easy for those watching it to make it worse, even to the extent of denying the fact it's happening at all.

'I can find no evidence for the alleged abusive tweets.'

Says someone sitting behind a computer. So not only can you be attacked but also the narrative is changed to deny that it ever happened at all. Twitter isn't reality, it's manipulated by those with the time and the power to make it whatever they want. It can be an isolating and lonely place and it is, without question, a dangerous world to inhabit at times.

Clementine Ford is a woman who, after receiving abuse on Facebook, reported the abuser to the troll's employees who decided after an investigation to sack him. She wrote about why she did it in an article for *Daily Life* in Australia and, to my mind, summarised brilliantly the Catch 22 situation that women find themselves in when face with trolls. She said:

- Here's how a typical interaction with the defenders and perpetrators of online abuse goes.

- 'Just block and delete them like a grownup!'

- *blocks and deletes*

- 'Oh so you're censoring people now? What, can't you handle debate?'

- *attempts to engage in a meaningful discussion, explaining why harassment is unacceptable*

- 'Get over it, it's just a word. I get called words all the time and I don't cry like a baby!'

- *loses temper resorts to name-calling*

- 'F—k you, you f—king whore. I should have known you'd resort to ad hominem attacks. You feminists are all the same, you just hate men because none of us will f—k you, fat dogs.'

Social media is like your annoying friend who stays sober and remembers everything anyone did on a drunken night out. Because it's not just you who is in charge of your digital footprint. I know that there are videos online of gigs I did years ago when I was, it's fair to say, awful. I've been tagged in photographs online that I don't even remember. Unlike the heady days of freedom when I was growing up, nowadays mistakes can haunt you forever. In my day I was absolutely able to do things that I regret, say things I didn't mean or wake up on a mattress in an alleyway after a drunken night out (I'm so proud of that one). But I did it and unless I tell you about it you'll never know. These days almost everything that we do is recorded somewhere in some way. We have no control of whether or not it's deleted or displayed in a Facebook account that we don't even know exists.

One of the particular characteristics of my depression is constantly rehashing events over and over again in my mind, wondering what I should have done, what I could have done, and how what I did has been perceived by others. Social media means that it's not just me that looks at what I do, others can freely comment on what I think. And it can be the most extraordinary thing to suddenly find yourself on the receiving end of an attack without realising what you did.

Here's a strange example. I like to start the week by posting an amusing animal picture. It makes me happy, and can often start the week for my followers on a positive note. I'd read that otters hold hands with their chosen partner otter when they sleep so they don't drift away from each other, which is adorable. I found a picture of two otters holding hands and posted it with the message: 'Otters hold hands when they're sleeping so they don't drift away from each other. Excuse me, I think I have something in my eye.' Innocuous. Or so I thought.

The day started in a normal fashion, a few retweets and some nice comments about how cheerful the little furry sweeties made people feel. Someone far more famous than myself also retweeted it and it snowballed. All was fine until I started getting a few strange comments, and I apologise for any offence anyone takes to this particular passage, I am merely recounting the story.

'Do you know Susan, that otters rape baby seals TO DEATH'. I'll admit I didn't. And I wasn't sure what I was meant to do with that information. I had simply posted a picture of some cute creatures. The comments that followed all contained two similar elements. Firstly, the information regarding the sexual assault of seals but almost all of them were addressed specifically to me. 'Do you know **Susan**' 'Are you aware **Susan**' 'I'm surprised at you **Susan**'. It seemed that some thought I was endorsing Baby Seal Rape and that as a good feminist my behaviour was essentially the equivalent, for the good people of Twitter, of saying I endorsed all types of rape. I was a wildlife rape apologist. It was a genuinely odd experience to be on the receiving end of an avalanche of tweets from strangers all round the world, all of whom were determined to make their voices heard against a bitch in Glasgow who wanted baby seals to be sexually abused. In that situation it's the personalisation of criticism that can make social media particularly difficult to cope with and especially so if you're already in a slightly delicate state.

Sometimes I feel that Twitter is the Crab of Hate multiplied by a million. And if you are feeling down about yourself it can be a bad place to be. Whenever I've had problems the most common things people tell me are:

'Why don't you come off Twitter if it's so bad?'

'Just ignore it.'

'You need to develop a thicker skin.'

I'll address each of those in turn. Firstly, that I should just stop being on Twitter if it's that bad. That's not really something I want to do because it's an excellent business tool that helps me let those who do enjoy what I do know when I'm touring or when I'm on the radio. But more than that, despite all of its failings, I really like social media. I love talking to people I wouldn't normally have contact with, of finding out new points of view and information about news all around the world. Watching comedy that's being made in different countries and chatting to like-minded *Buffy the Vampire Slayer* fans in time zones far removed from mine. I'm also very stubborn. To leave Twitter (and I have occasionally thought about it) would be to let those who want to shut down other points of view win.

Secondly, the easy option of just ignoring it. That's usually the line from someone who has twelve followers and who does nothing apart from RT Ellen DeGeneres occasionally. It's hard to ignore it; it's hard to let people talk about you when you want them to stop. It's the powerless feeling that I had when I was younger of not being able to control what's happening. Of course, you can just ignore it if you aren't actually online, but as I said before, I am in charge of my Twitter account. It's me on the other end of the computer.

Lastly, that I need to develop a thicker skin. I can't tell you how many times I've been told that throughout my life. But it's tough. Part of understanding the Crab of Hate is understanding me, and I know what I am. I have skin that is like wet rice paper. If you grab me too hard you'll rip right through it. I have a very thin skin, and the only person who gets hurt by it is me.

I'm not happy about the fact that I have, over time, become calloused by online interactions, that my personality has been fundamentally altered by what I initially thought was a fun thing to be involved in. I've even come up with a series of rules that I implement to keep myself and my head safe on social media:

1. *Never post a picture of an otter.* Ever. No matter how cute you think they are. It's not worth it. See also anything to do with Piers Morgan.

2. *If you think someone has insulted you they probably have.* Block them. The first few times you do this you may worry about being so harsh. Don't. Block, block and block again. I also block people who I see making negative comments about friends. Oftentimes people will contact my agent asking why I blocked them, usually it's because you called my friend fat. I don't like you.

3. Don't feed the trolls. You will probably have heard this saying on many occasions, the meaning of which is to ignore those who send abuse because they feed off knowing that they've hit their mark and upset you. I have to say I agree with it. There are some peculiar folks out there that delight in knowing that someone else in the world is crying because of something that they've done. Don't give them the pleasure.

4. Never google yourself. I certainly don't. To do so would be the equivalent of rubbing salt and lemon into a paper cut.

5. Follow people who make you happy. If your timeline is full of things that make you angry, change things up. Immediately defriend people on Facebook who are passive aggressive or upset you. If I switch on my computer and see a status update that makes me uncomfortable, then they're gone. A real friend will never try to make you feel awful about yourself, a real friend stands up for you and makes you feel fabulous. Get rid of the online idiots who make the Crab of Hate happy.

6. Pick your fights carefully. The Internet is full of people whose only role in life is to make people miserable.

7. Kittens. When I feel like things are getting too much for me and Twitter is too negative for my liking I post a picture of a kitten or a puppy (NOT AN OTTER, I REPEAT NOT AN OTTER).

8. *Never ever post in anger.* I often write tweets and then walk away from my computer for a good hour, and then return and reread what I've said. On most occasions I've calmed down and realised that it's not appropriate to send it.

9. *Don't be a hypocrite.* If you dislike the way that people are treated online, don't join in when a friend or a celeb is slagging someone off. We all have a responsibility to make the place better. Do your bit.

10. *I try to remember this.* I am liked by many, not liked by some, but loved by those who matter. This is the most important thing. Social media is not the real world although it can feel as important. Make sure you take time off and enjoy conversations or outings that really mean something.

Certainly for me, the internet is a wonderful place that makes me feel far less isolated and more normal. But it can be awful. Be careful about what you post and who you interact with. And if you are in trouble, switch off your computer and spend some time with actual human beings.

CHAPTER 13

THE WAY WE LOOK TONIGHT:
DRESSING FOR SUCCESS

IN the previous chapter I talked about some of the comments I've received on social media about the way that I look. I find these some of the most difficult to deal with because there's only so much that I can do to change my appearance. All my life I've been uncomfortable with the way I look but I have, over a long period of time, come to accept that embracing my individuality has enabled me, finally, to be a bit more proud of what I look like.

This doesn't sound like a startling revelation but as Rocky Balboa probably didn't say 'I didn't know I had a problem until I was punched in the face. Adrian!' I've always been told that looking better makes you feel better, but I thought that was a shallow position to take. I was certain that it was wrong to judge people by their appearance and so kicked against it. I had a dream that one day a woman would not be judged by the Louboutins they wore, but by the content of their character.

I know. You're shouting out loud, 'Everyone wants that

Susan, are you some form of idiot?' Why yes. Yes I am. For example, it took years for me to accept that a full acid perm did **not** make me look like Whitney Houston.

I know that most people wouldn't like to admit that they judge others by how they look, but it's human nature, even if we fight that natural inclination. Science has apparently proven that we decide what we think about someone within the first ten seconds of meeting them. As a stand-up comedian, I know that those first few seconds on stage are the most crucial, as an audience will judge me, at least initially, on how I look, not on what I say. That's just a microcosm for life. You may not jump up on stage every night, but it happens to all of us every day. If you're reading this book right now on the train, or in a coffee shop you might well be looking at the people around you. And judging them.

Of course, having an issue with how we look isn't a new concept. I'm sure cavewomen compared themselves unfavourably to their neighbours. Especially if those neighbours looked like Raquel Welch. But the pressure on all of us to look good and feel great has increased in modern times. I hesitate to suggest it, as it's an easy target, but I do think that the media doesn't help. The vast array of makeover shows, even when dressed up as 'lifestyle' programmes, are essentially selling the idea that complying with society's notion of fashion and trends will make you happier with your appearance. Shows like *10 Years Younger*, *Tart Me Up* and *How to look good for one show then never dress like that again* perpetuate the problems.

I'd be perfect for one of those shows, although the idea

of Gok Wan rummaging around my lady chest area makes me break out in a sweat. I'm extremely awkward when it comes to such things. In fact, my top three most awkward moments in fashion that have actually happened to me are, in no particular order:

1. A bra fitting where, after removing my T-shirt, I realised that I'd forgotten to shave my armpits and I'd accidentally worn my gardening bra. In case you're wondering, a gardening bra is the equivalent of a gardening jumper. Full of holes, and it doesn't matter if it gets muddy.

2. Hiring a personal shopper to try and help me improve my fashion sense only to have her give up after an hour because I was too difficult.

3. Attempting to buy sexy underwear to spice things up in the bedroom and, when approached by a sales assistant, suddenly panicking, shouting 'my pants will have to do' and running out the door, only to have to return to the shop moments later to retrieve my rucksack that I'd left on the floor.

I've never had much confidence in the way that I look. I know that I don't look like I live under a bridge or anything, nor am I the kind of person that Channel 5 will make a documentary about with the subtitle 'The woman whose face looked like a Brussels sprout', but I've always wanted to look very different from the way that I actually do. So for most of my life I pretended that I didn't care about my appearance. A combination of lack of innate style, money, confidence and a body-shape equivalent of a Weeble (we wobble but we don't fall down!) meant that it was just easier not to bother at all.

When trying to describe what I was like when I was younger, I wish I had a time machine so I could show you what I used to be like rather than just describe it. But it's unlikely that I could invent such a thing, given that I was recently unable to work the toilet lock on a train. To the gentleman who opened the door on me that day, I can only apologise again.

So you'll just have to imagine the year 1984. If you were there you'll know what it was about. Look at the hair! Look at the clothes! The horror! The humanity! The reason that we are here at this specific time is because, in 1984, a very young Calman found her first fashion idol. I was ten, and if you wanted to find me the best place to look was my granny's house. My gran was a fabulous woman who, when she was younger, worked as a secretary at the House of Fraser. But that's not what she really wanted to be. Because when she was younger my granny wanted to be glamorous. She's sadly passed away now but I remember her every day even in little ways. I still have her recipe for ice cream. What you do is you get a tin of Carnation milk, pour it into a bowl and then freeze it. *Masterchef* here I come.

When we weren't making gourmet food together we would spend our afternoons watching old movies, and it's from this time that I get my love of film stars like Doris Day, Bette Davis and Greta Garbo. We would watch classics like *Ninotchka* and *The Thin Man*, and my gran would tell me that when she was a girl she'd wanted to be a movie star. And she was absolutely convinced that if she hadn't been born in Glasgow she would've made it. While I loved all of the old time stars, one woman, who was to me the epitome of glamour and beauty, entranced me. Marlene Dietrich. We would watch *Destry Rides Again* and *The Blue Angel* and my gran would say to me, with absolute sincerity: 'When you grow up, you can be just like Marlene Dietrich.' I'd look at her with wide eyes and say, 'Can I? Can I really?' And she would nod, take another spoon of ice cream and nod again. That's quite a role model to have in your head. It's also a quite sexually confusing woman for me to emulate. Half the time Dietrich was dressed in a top hat and tails, which I'm fairly sure contributed to my desire to dress like Fred Astaire rather than Ginger Rogers.

The main obstacle to this dream becoming a reality was, quite simply, me. I couldn't glide across a room. I couldn't even wear anything white because by the time I got to the front door I'd be covered in dirt. When I was younger my nickname was 'Pig Pen' which was slightly nicer than the nickname my brother gave me which was 'Smelly Tights Calman'. It's a shame, life isn't like the treasured childhood television programme *Mr Benn*, you can't walk into a changing room and leave as someone else. If life were like that I'd imagine everyone would be happier. Dull office meetings would be much more fun if you were sitting beside a cowboy, a spaceman and your boss was dressed as a tiger.

My dream to be La Dietrich crashed when I realised what a duff hand life had dealt me. Firstly, and most importantly, I have no sense of style. I wear clothes because to do otherwise would be upsetting and, let's face it, chilly. I live in Glasgow. Everyday nudity would lead to an awful lot of chaffing. Even in the height of summer.

My lack of fashion sense is, I believe, my parents' fault. But then, what isn't? I often feel bad for blaming them for all of my problems, but then I remember that's the price you pay for having such a ray of sunshine lighting up the gloom of your everyday existence. In my mind, for most of us, fashion has four separate phases in life. Phase one, you're dressed by your parents and have little say in what you wear. Phase two, you leave home and dress yourself. Phase three, you meet someone, fall in love, and compromise your sense of style to 'prevent embarrassment'. You know when your partner doesn't like what you wear and slowly, but surely, starts 'accidentally' shrinking or disposing of all of the things you had before you met them and replacing them with things they want you to wear. I had a Wham! scarf that ended up as a pan scourer. And then there's the final phase. When you're too old to worry about anything anymore and someone dresses you. It's the circle of life courtesy of Marks and Spencer.

Phase one, when clothing is chosen for you, is perhaps the most crucial phase in our fashion development as it forms our early perceptions of style. As I've said, for the most part you're made to dress for whatever occasion you're forced to attend in accordance with your parents' view of what's appropriate. To be fair to my mum, I was a girl and there are certain societal pressures to dress girls in a certain way. As a result, I often found myself forcibly restrained by the many sequins and ribbons on a pretty party dress, constricted in a bejewelled straitjacket. Not that it had the desired effect of making me more girly. As a child, when wearing said pretty party dress, I usually resembled an angry hobbit at a Halloween party. In truth the early eighties were my fashion Vietnam. Once I wore a pink, silk flying suit and pixie boots to a friend's birthday party. I'll just give you a moment to picture this. I've woken on many nights silently screaming as a result of that outfit. No wonder. I looked like Penelope Pitstop if she'd been squashed in an industrial accident.

My mum did try her best, bless her. She bought me a special outfit for the school disco once. She went into a shop called Tammy Girl, which many of you will remember with fondness. It's like Primark but with more dignity. In the eighties there was very much a fashion for everything matching exactly. Not like now when you buy separate pieces of clothing that will go together. She chose for me a polka dot outfit. A batwing cardigan and culottes. If you don't know what culottes are, they're not trousers, they're not a skirt, they're one of the most unflattering items known to man. I didn't get asked for a dance, I'm not surprised. I looked like a jockey dressed as MC Hammer. She may as well have put a sign on me that said 'Don't touch this', and no one did.

I was the youngest of three children. Which means that I was cursed by the 'hand me down'. I know that it's financially better to reuse the clothes that your other children have worn, and that it's excessive to buy all of your offspring clothes that suit them. But for the child in the unfortunate position of being the youngest, it can result in what can only be described as a schizophrenic attitude to apparel. I wore my brother's old clothes, comprising eighties' army jumpers and football tops. I wore my sister's old clothes, which, as she was the epitome of femininity, were puffball skirts and snoods. I veered between Molly Ringwald in *The Breakfast Club* and Sylvester Stallone in *Rambo*. I was half boy/half girl. A sexually confused transformer child who was becoming more like Marlene Dietrich every day. When it came to clothes anyway.

Even on the rare occasions where I was allowed to choose my own clothes, the result was disastrous. When I tried to join in what was 'on trend', I couldn't. If there's one thing I'm not, it's 'on trend'. I'm very much off trend. If the trend is, metaphorically, France, I'm in Caracas, Venezuela.

The eighties, when I was teenager, was a nightmare of rah-rah skirts legwarmers and blue eyeshadow. I was trying to emulate the icons of the time like Madonna, Cyndi Lauper and Hazell Dean, but it just didn't fit who I was inside. I was like one of those weird Heston Blumenthal dishes that looks like an orange but actually contains chicken pâté. I was trying to look like an eighties' diva but, inside, I was Sid James.

The next phase in my fashion evolution was when I left home to go to university. It started badly when I moved into halls of residence. There's always a certain amount of concern about who you'll be sharing a room with, and for me it was even more pressing, given my lack of confidence. I'd splashed out to buy a pair of cherry Doc Martens that I'd been told were essential for any hip young thing. Being a size three, however, they resembled shoes one might wear to correct a foot defect. I told myself that it would be fine, and posed the eternal question, *What's the worst that could happen?* Well, the worst that could happen was the unlikely event that my roommate would be a six-foot-tall model. And that's what happened. My roommate *was* a six-foot-tall model. We looked like Danny DeVito and Arnold Schwarzenegger in *Twins*.

These years when one leaves school and takes the first faltering steps into adulthood, whether spent at university or not, is the time when many young people find their identity. They find a way to express themselves through their clothes. The Goths, the rockers, the preppy group. But when I finally got the freedom I'd wanted, I didn't feel excitement at all. The only way I can describe how I felt being free to choose my own clothes for the first time is . . . uncomfortable. A feeling of dread, comparable to the one you get when you can't remember what you did on a night out but you've woken up chained to the office junior and you appear to have matching Black Sabbath tattoos.

The most pressing issue I have with the way that I look, and one that became increasingly obvious to me as I stood next to a model every morning, is the body that I've been stuck with. They say a poor workman never blames his tools, but when you're trapped in the body of a twelve-year-old there's not a lot you can do. Apart from panto.

I've always been short, but I've never really got used to it. My recurring dream is to be of average height, not really tall, just tall enough to reach the shelves in supermarkets without asking for help. I'm four foot eleven, although my wife suggests I may be exaggerating. She says I'm four foot ten. It's quite hideous to think that saying I'm four foot eleven is an exaggeration. I'm the same height as Kylie Minogue, you know. I have one talent being this short, it's outstanding. I can stand up completely straight in the back of a black cab. It's quite an expensive hobby but I enjoy it.

I'm short and I'm stocky, or as my gran described me, healthy. Let's just say that I'm the kind of person who'll survive the next ice age without much of a problem. But it's not just that, I have odd dimensions. Short legs and an unfeasibly high waist. I remember being reassured when I read Judy Garland's biography. She, like me, was four foot eleven. And like me her waist started at her shoulders.

Being short causes more problems than you might think. Everything is out of proportion. The waistband of jackets is at my hips. Shoulders are too big and if I try to buy petite clothing it doesn't fit. For some reason shops seem to think short equals thin, that proportionally tiny people are more skinny.

I'm required, on average, to cut seven inches off the bottom of a pair of trousers when I buy them. When I was at university I hadn't yet discovered the joy of Wundaweb and so simply bought old pairs of Levi's and cut them with a pair of scissors. The frayed edges gave me the look of a scarecrow that had let itself go a bit.

Despite really, really wanting to look like a film star, I just couldn't. I didn't have the money, I didn't have the confidence. I didn't have the body. It was easier to fall back on a tried and trusted friend.

So I decided to make it not about looking good, but to make it a political statement. In my experience you can justify almost everything with politics except, oddly enough, politics. And so rather than address the fact that I was an awkward looking, oddly shaped human being with no real sense of style, I used dogma as an excuse to hide in my clothes and make myself as unattractive and unfeminine as I could.

You see, when I was at university I encountered, for the first time, gender politics. Now, I'm aware that the attempt to summarise gender politics and make it funny within the confines of this book is as easy as washing a cat in the kitchen sink, and that no doubt some of you will disagree with what I say. But remember this is my recollection. In the same way as victory is rewritten by the victors, my life is written from a shorter perspective than you might remember.

There was a political stance at that time, born largely out of the post-punk/1970s version of feminism, which I went along with, which was that to feminise yourself was to buy into the misogynistic patriarchy that oppresses women and enslaves them in a traditional culture of child-rearing followed by a slow death by ironing. It was a laugh a minute back then. Honestly.

There's something tremendously reassuring about knowing that if people criticise you for something, you can explain your conduct away by saying 'actually I wasn't trying in the first place'. So I pierced my nose, I wore an old army coat, I shaved the back of my head. I decided that if I wasn't going to be noticed for being attractive, if I wasn't going to turn heads when I entered the room because of how lovely I looked, I would be the exact opposite. I stomped around campus with my DM boots embracing the idea that I didn't want to be attractive. That those who judged me for how I looked on the outside weren't worth talking to.

But it wasn't actually the clothes that were the problem. It was the bit inside the clothes. It was me. I didn't like me. And I particularly didn't like how much there was of me. Like many people, I've always had issues with my weight. In fact, the only time I've ever lost a lot of weight was when I was dumped by my first love. I didn't eat, I didn't sleep. I was thin. And I was miserable. I'm a textbook comfort eater and it becomes a vicious circle. Why go out and socialise when you can eat a Viennetta with your hands. A Viennetta won't sleep with your best friend will it? Or come round and take your N64 and GoldenEye, one of the best video games ever made. Am I right, gamers?

After the awkward years of my early twenties, I became a lawyer. I wore suits that gave me the look of a member of the Lollipop Guild. I'll tell you this story that may help you understand why I gave up being a lawyer. I was working in a shiny corporate firm and was posted to the Edinburgh office. This meant travelling from Glasgow to the capital on the train every day in a three hour door-to-door commute. Part of being a young lawyer was turning up extra early for morning meetings so I could make the coffee and get the partners their cherry scones and such like. I was leaving my house, in the wintertime, at about 6.15 a.m., in the cold and the rain. I have always been keen on comfort and even more so when trudging round shops in Edinburgh to get an arsehole his cherry scone. So I wore a trouser suit (an expensive one, mind) and a pair of Tank Girl boots that I would change out of when I got to the office. After a few weeks of travelling and looking more and more dishevelled as the long nights and early mornings took their toll, I was called into the senior partner's office for a chat. He sat me down and said, and I'm paraphrasing here:

'Don't you think you'd do better, Susan, if you just made more of an effort. Perhaps wore a skirt, or some lipstick.'

I'll be honest, dear reader, I was dumbstruck. This was the late nineties to be fair, but really. I'm surprised he didn't suggest I dress up in a nurse's uniform and run round the park accompanied by the theme tune to Benny Hill. This is the one and only time in my early life when I actually stood up for myself, I think because I was so shocked at the suggestion that I needed to look more like a woman in order to get on. I asked the partner, politely I like to think, whether or not he would have asked one of the men in the office to change the way that they looked in order to get on in the office. Perhaps one of the young lawyers who insisted on having long hair in a desperate effort to look like Liam Gallagher. I was simply told that it was different for women and I had to suck it up and deal with it. Wear a skirt, wear some make-up, get on in life. Don't worry about the men, they're men and they can do whatever they want.

I was just as miserable as always and, one fatal day, made the decision to give up my job to become a comedian. As I've said before, some people often say it was a brave decision, others suggest I was an idiot. Which, remembering I wanted to look like Whitney Houston, I am. But one of the attractions of the new career was that I genuinely thought no one would care what I looked like as long as I made them laugh. Which was, in fact, the biggest mistake of my life. Apart from when I entered my cats into *Britain's Got Talent* with our acrobatic troupe 'The Catrobats'. Then I discovered that no one wants to see a grown woman, wearing a leotard, covered in tuna, crying as three cats sleep in front of her.

I learned very quickly when I started doing stand-up that it's fairly standard for comedians to make an immediate joke, as soon as they step on stage, about a celebrity that they look like. You may have seen a comic doing this but not understood why it's such an accepted trope in the humour business. To be frank, one of the main reasons we do it is so that the audience doesn't do it for us. When gigging in Scotland it's just easier to make a Jimmy Krankie joke myself rather than have someone shout 'Fandabidozi' at me five minutes later. And personally I find that modern references are easier for an audience to connect with than comparing myself to other famous short people. Although now I'm on Radio 4, more people get my Toulouse-Lautrec references than they did previously.

After a few years on the stand-up circuit I found myself making my first foray into the world of television, and it was at that point that I realised just how important the looks of a lady comic are. Not just to the audience but also to the people making the shows. Gentlemen have faces full of character that don't require more than the merest suggestion of powder to take the sheen off their cheeks. Women have faces that need covering in a pile of plaster before they can be seen by millions in their living rooms. Television is obsessed with a particular idea of women. And it seems that their idea of the perfect woman is a woman who is caked in so much make up that when she smiles large cracks appear in her façade.

The more I appeared on television, the more the pressure rose. My face was suddenly being beamed to millions in their living rooms. I had to get used to something that I hadn't encountered before. The art of being made to look beautiful.

The first time I appeared on television I had no idea the work that would be required to make me look acceptable. When the make-up department asked me how I wanted to look, I said just make me look natural. Sadly, natural for me looks like a jaundiced panda and that's not going to make anyone feel happy watching at home. So they painted me, they smoothed out my spots, and they made me look like someone else. I didn't feel like myself, it was like I was a pod person from *Invasion of the Body Snatchers* and the real me was locked in a cupboard somewhere.

But the more I transformed into their idea of a woman, the less like me I felt. I still didn't think it suited me to make an effort, I was happier when I resembled someone who had slept in a hedge. No matter how unhappy I was, I clung on to my shtick that I didn't care. I should be judged on who I was, not how I looked. And I was as sure of that view as I am of the fact that, no matter what the snobs at university said to me, tinned potato salad is a valid tapas dish.

But then something rather unexpected happened. I visited Berlin with my better half for a city break (her choice, not mine). Not that I don't like the country, I just don't speak the language. My better half is fluent in German and had a lovely time during our visit there. As is my way, I became frustrated with being unable to ask for anything apart from 'sausages and beer please' and ended up making up German words in the hope they would catch on. Applepumpfen was my favourite. If you hear that in Berlin you know where it came from.

We were in Berlin, in the middle of winter and I was miserable. In order to cheer me up it was suggested we visit a museum. Woohoo! Why not suggest some time at an art gallery to get the party really started? But in an effort to seem less like the least cheerful of the seven dwarfs, I acceded to the cultural request. We wandered round, as one does in a museum, looking forward to visiting the gift shop to buy a mug. I always buy a mug when I visit anywhere. I even bought one when I stopped to use the facilities at Tebay services. It has a sheep on it. My mood lifted as we made our way to mug paradise, when we saw a room we hadn't visited yet. It was packed with display cases filled with clothes and top hats and slowly, but surely, I realised what I was looking at. It was a shrine to one woman. Marlene Dietrich. I stood, transfixed.

What struck me most was her height. I'd always imagined that Dietrich was tall and willowy. She certainly looked that way on screen. But looking at the clothes she wore it was clear that, while she was still taller than me (who isn't?), she wasn't a six-foot-tall Amazon. She was about five foot five, not stick thin by any manner of means, but the way she held herself made her look six foot tall. She was a real, shortish woman. Just like me.

I made a decision to start trying. Why? Because I'd had enough. Because I'd had my road to Damascus moment and all because I'd seen Marlene's clothes. And because of an incident with a friend of mine about a week before we went on holiday. I'd decided to buy a pair of bright pink capri pants. I'm still not completely clear why, but I remember thinking at the time that they looked pretty ace. I wore them to lunch and when I met my friend, she laughed at me. Just laughed at me. I went bright pink, to match the trousers, and went home and changed. I realised that Marlene wouldn't have gone home and changed, she would've stuck a bow on her behind and called herself a birthday present. I was gradually inching out of the fashion closet as a tiny, Scottish Dietrich.

I didn't think dressing in a top hat and tails would work for everyday wear, at the very least it would be awkward on the Tube, but I decided that instead of fighting against my natural inclination not to dress like a girl I should embrace it. I bought tweed waistcoats, herringbone-pattern trousers, shirts and jackets with patches on the elbow. I looked like a gentleman from the 1920s and it felt amazing.

Not long after our visit to Berlin, I got a chance to try out my new style. I've always wanted to go on the Orient Express, mainly because I once saw the film *Murder on the Orient Express*. Which is a stupid reason to go on a holiday. 'Oh look someone got stabbed on that train! Let's go for a wee break!' It's like watching Taggart and thinking, *Glasgow looks friendly*. I was so very excited about the trip, but then I realised, very quickly, that it was completely out with my social comfort zone.

The reason I knew that there might be an issue was because, before we left for Venice, through the letterbox dropped a novel-sized dress code and etiquette guide. It said that on board the Orient Express you weren't allowed to wear jeans, trainers or T-shirts. That's OK, I have other clothes. I mean they're pyjamas but they are still technically clothes. It said that there is no such thing as too glamorous on board the Orient Express. There is. It's me. Anyway, we panicked for a bit and then we thought, *To hell with it*. In for a penny and in for a pound. So we bought tuxedos. My wife had a white one and I got a black one, and a monocle and pipe. And we burst into the bar carriage, 'Hello, we're the leshbians in carriage B!' I don't know why I spoke like Sean Connery. It just seemed appropriate.

It's the only time in my life where my ability to play bridge has come in useful. You may be asking yourself, how the hell do you know how to play bridge Susan? I'll tell you. When I was at school I did the Duke of Edinburgh awards scheme, and I chose, as my skill, bridge. I remember sitting in bridge club at the age of thirteen and thinking, 'I'll never use this'. Then, sitting on the Orient Express, wearing a top hat, shouting, 'Another rubber, Colonel?'

Now that's what I'm talking about. Once I embraced the idea that style doesn't have to be what we're told it is in magazines or on television, it made sense. Basically, what's on the outside now matches what's on the inside. I'm not conforming to social stereotypes, I'm finally dressing the way I want to. Yes, it's taken me twenty years longer than most people to find out what I want to look like, but I know now.

I finally feel comfortable with myself. I don't mind when people laugh at me in my tweed suits. And I genuinely don't care that a woman of my stature should probably wear heels to give herself a bit of extra height. I'm sticking with my brogues. Partly because I have plantar fasciitis.

I still think my younger self was right, you shouldn't be judged on your outward appearance. But the reality is that we are. So you have two options. You can shrink into the shrubbery of life, camouflaging yourself in the hope of avoiding the worst of the stares. Or you can accept that the harshest critic you'll ever encounter is yourself, and go for it.

You may not agree with what I've said, but that's fine. I'm a miniature Marlene Dietrich from Glasgow and, darling, I look fabulous.

CHAPTER 14
MAYBE IT IS YOUR FAULT:
WHODUNNIT?

SOMETIMES I feel a bit like Miss Marple, not least because of my fondness for a tweed cape. I love a whodunit; I love trying to work out who killed whom with what in which room of a mansion in a detective novel. And I apply that firm belief that I'm as good as a spinster from St Mary Mead to my own life, trying to work out, metaphorically, whodunit to me. Who gave me this eternal curse of depression. Like a good detective, I've made a shortlist of suspects:

1. *My mum and dad.* Easy target, but let's face it, it's bound to be their fault. Stupid people with their unwavering love and support and all of that idiotic nonsense. No wonder I'm a mess!

2. *School.* I clearly wasn't appreciated or nurtured enough by my teachers. My peers also couldn't cope with my brilliance and so bullied me relentlessly, leading to my lack of self-esteem.

3. *The media.* Of course it's their fault! I'm bombarded every day with pictures of thin, happy people who have no problems at all about anything.

4. *My ex-girlfriends.* It wasn't my fault that our relationships broke up! It was them. They just didn't understand me.

5. *The Church.* Stupid bigoted religion making me feel bad about myself.

6. *Politicians.* They just make me angry sometimes.

These are all plausible suspects, but the list is, of course, missing one crucial culprit. Me. Maybe some of this is my fault. Maybe I should be at the very top of the list. And before you all start metaphorically jumping down my throat, hear me out.

I'm constantly calling people out if they don't acknowledge how badly they treat me, so surely I should do the same for myself? Surely I should analyse how I live my life to see if there are things that I need to take responsibility for? To ask myself the perfectly reasonable question – are there things that I do or say which are less than helpful in getting myself to better mental health? And objectively the answer to all of these questions is undoubtedly yes. Difficult as this chapter is to write, it's important to be honest with myself and with you. And perhaps, if you recognise any of these behaviours then maybe, just maybe, it might also be, just a little bit, your fault as well.

After a great deal of ruminating late at night, I've distilled 'myself blame' theories into three distinct areas of concern.

1. Not everyone thinks about us as much as we think they do.

2. People can't read minds.

3. We need to give people a bit of a break.

Some bold propositions but ones that need to be examined. The first one in particular, that not everyone thinks about us as much as we think about us, is crucial to the paranoid, anxious part of my brain. You see, I think about 'me' a lot. How am *I*, what do people think about *me*, does anyone care about *me*, why am *I* not getting the same jobs other people get, why aren't people more considerate of *my* feelings? I am, at times, the very definition of *Me*, *Myself* and *I*. And the simple answer is that other people have their own lives, jobs, friends, problems. We may be an important part of their lives but they have their own insecurities and responsibilities to deal with. I've found myself leaving an event or a party paralysed with fear because of something that I've said, and spent the next couple of days worrying about what people would think of me. Of course, in reality, the hundred or so people who were at the event didn't spend the hour after I left the party talking about me. Despite what I might believe, I am not the planet around which everyone else orbits.

Not everyone is obsessed with what I do or what I say. A lot of paranoia is based around the assumption that what we say is the most important thing that could ever happen in the world at any time. That when I leave a room it's like all of the joy and fun has been sucked out of the world, and those who are left are compelled by the sheer force of my personality to talk constantly about me, and what I said and did.

It's not like that though, is it? We are just one person in a swamp of billions. One of my friends has a lovely way of putting it. She says, 'Get over yourself.' Quite right.

Secondly, people are not mind readers. Not even Derren Brown and he's brilliant. Some people are more attuned to body language and reading physical signs, which can lead to the suspicion that they can zero in on our very thoughts, but they can't. And let's face it, that's probably a good thing, otherwise my wife would never let me watch anything Gillian Anderson is in ever again. Sometimes the thoughts in my head are so loud and violent that it's difficult to believe that someone looking at me wouldn't know what I'm saying. Our internal monologue may be going twenty to the dozen but no one can possibly know that unless we tell them.

This realisation is a particularly key part of my more recent successful coping mechanisms that I've implemented with my wife. I am pretty uncomfortable in social situations, even more so now that people can often recognise me from the television. People think that I'm a tremendously gregarious outgoing person but the reality is I'm quite shy. If I know I'm going to a new place with people I don't know, I can often panic and react badly. For a few years my wife had no idea why I was often reluctant, angry in fact, when we were in pubs or clubs. I would simply sulk in the corner or refuse to go out at all. The panic in my head was screaming at such a loud volume that I couldn't understand why she didn't know what the problem was. But she couldn't, because she's not a mind reader. And so I had to sit her down and verbalise my fears, tell her what was in my head. And now we have a system. She will check I'm OK, and stay with me until I feel comfortable enough with where I am and who I'm with. We also have a safe word, which is 'penguin', and when that's uttered we make a quick exit.

But I had to actually tell her. I know it's frustrating when you have to take the time to empty your head, but it's essential to allow those who are close to you to help. You can't get angry with friends or colleagues for not dealing with your depression the way you'd like them to when they don't know how you're feeling. Even if they happen to be a fellow DWB member you must remember my first point in this exercise of taking responsibility. Not everyone thinks about us as much as we think about us. When meeting a friend for a cuppa, there's no point in getting angry that they don't immediately ask you how you're doing or don't remember what you told them last time you talked. Did you ask them how they were?

And that brings us to point three. Those of us living with depression need to give people a bit of a break. Not everyone is excellent at dealing with even the slightest flicker of emotion, never mind someone emptying their head onto their lap. I'm pretty sure I've lost friends because of my own stupidity or resentment that they're not treating me the right way. I can only imagine how frightening it must have been for friends of mine, when I was younger, for me to tell them I was self-harming and had had thoughts of suicide. I was selfish, in fact, not to think of what a responsibility they must have felt being confronted with that kind of threat. I may have rehearsed the conversations in my mind over and over again, but they haven't. 'If they don't react the way that I want them to then we're through' is a good way of ending up with no one. Of course, no one should put up with inappropriate behaviour from someone we have confided in, but in the same way as we might want people to give us a chance, we need to provide the same courtesy to others.

It's a difficult question to ask, but 'is there something I can do to make myself feel better?' For years I've avoided doing anything proactive which might help my mental health. But recently I started taking more responsibility for my own head. As I've said before, I don't drink as much as I used to. I've stopped smoking (which was a remarkable instance of self-harm that I continued for twenty years) and, more than that, I've stopped dismissing suggestions from friends and started opening my mind to new possibilities.

It's often said that taking some sort of exercise helps mental health, but it always seemed to me that the people who suggested it were the kind of people who enjoyed exercise in the first place. Whenever someone suggested a trip to the gym I was transported back to a time in my life when I was miserable. When I had to take part in cross-country running at school. Running round and round a park for no discernible reason in pants and a vest. I've always been a bit of a philosopher, you see, or as my teachers at school called me, difficult. When asked to run round the park three times I asked what I thought was a reasonable question, which was, 'Why?' Only to be told that there was no reason. To which I replied that if there was no reason then why do it? My PE teacher was unwilling to indulge in philosophical debates of this nature and instead told me if I didn't run quickly I'd have to do it four times. Which is a sadistic, but effective, way of encouraging someone to do something they don't want to. And so every time I tried to take some exercise I end up back in the position of that child running for hours neither to, nor from, anything. I can honestly say that there has never been a time when I've been more depressed than when I was exercising.

But that's pretty standard for me, to be dismissive of a potential solution because of a childhood trauma or, more likely, because it sounds like a lot of hard work. The bottom line is that there's quite compelling evidence that getting off the sofa and moving around can really help. If you were to ask me to isolate what the main reason for my own feelings of self-hatred are, I'd say it's the way that I look. On the rare occasions that I look in the mirror all I see is a short, fat, horrific monster. And I've always felt big and lumbering. I've never liked having my picture taken or any social situation where my appearance might be critiqued.

I may have mentioned this particular depression trigger to my wife a few hundred times, and one day she snapped. She quite rightly said that the way I looked was something we could do something about. But it would require positive action. She tentatively suggested that we should get a personal trainer. Even though that sounded pretty awful I agreed that drastic action was needed.

We decided to start our search at our local council facility, called the Glasgow Club. We made an appointment and found that we could hire a personal trainer and also attend the classes for free if we paid a yearly subscription. And we did. And we got a personal trainer. A lovely man called Mark, because we both agreed that having a boy shout at us would be a nice change and quite funny. And he's wonderful. It sounds terribly LA and lazy to need someone to motivate me, but it works. He doesn't criticise us, never suggests that our lack of fitness is our own fault, and he pushes us in a way I never thought possible.

Now on an average week we complete at least five classes, usually so high intensity that they're vomit inducing. Once a week the personal trainer takes us through an hour of weight training and cardio, meaning that I'm usually in bed exhausted by 10 p.m. every night. Thursdays and Saturdays are days off for recovery, but I miss the feeling that I get from exercising. When I found out that my local gym was closed for four days over Christmas, I was angry that I wouldn't be able to have fun for such a sustained period of time.

The loss of inches is slow (as it should be), but is definitely happening. But more than that, I love the feeling of getting fitter, healthier and happier. The staff at the Glasgow Club have been incredibly helpful, my fellow gym goers are supportive and each class we've gone to has been clearly explained and safely demonstrated.

I've become evangelical about it all. I'm now the person I used to hate, trying to persuade my friends to get fit, to join me in the early morning to sweat with a group of strangers.

But most importantly it really, REALLY, helps my mental health. The fact that I'm proactively doing something about something that makes me feel miserable is amazing. And it's encouraging me to take more pride in who I am and how I look. I know that I'll never look like a model in a magazine, but I can make the best of what I have. It provides me with an hour every day when I can't think about all of the things that are annoying me because I have to concentrate on something else. It gives me a break from the insular way that I sometimes think. I can feel myself becoming fitter, it encourages me to eat more healthily and take care of myself. The hatred I felt for myself when I would spend the weekend recovering from a drinking session and eating takeaways is gone.

No one else can take these steps for me, I have to get up, get out of my house and go to the gym. I have to admit that there are things I can do to make me feel better. Me, myself and I.

CHAPTER 15

RELATIONSHIPS:
DATING

HUMAN beings do not, as a general rule, live in a vacuum. Although there are times when I think that might be nice. The mornings when I've woken up and just can't face pretending to be normal, when all I want to do is hide in my homemade bunker with the cats. Those times are rare, and more often than not I crave company, sometimes desperately. Loneliness and anxiety are key feelings that can arise when depressed, and I have at times made bad choices when it comes to friends and relationships, so panicked was I about being left on my own. I'm in a good place now, in fact I even managed to find someone to marry me, but my choices have sometimes been, how should I put it, horrific.

When I was in the darkest days of my depression, the times when the Crab of Hate was jauntily tap dancing on my shoulder every day, I didn't think enough of myself to believe that anyone would actually want to spend any quality time with me. Friends were people whom I spent time with rather than had any real connection with, and I was so desperate not to drive them away that I didn't reveal how truly awful I felt to them. Certainly in my early twenties, the people that I knew were fixated on clubbing and drinking and drugs rather than spending time doing anything in the daytime. I pretended to fit in, but I didn't. I hate drugs. I don't need any help feeling paranoid so the idea of paying money for the privilege seemed quite absurd.

I wasn't confident enough at that point in my life to see that the time spent in such places was actually more negative than just staying in the house by myself. One of the peculiarities of being gay in a relatively small place like Glasgow (certainly in the 1990s) was that pubs and clubs were really the only environment in which you could meet potential partners. And I so longed to have a girlfriend! Someone to love who would love me back and we would go to Ikea and dress in identical Pac A Macs! For a time I truly believed that finding a partner would cure me of my depression, that all I needed to feel better about myself was to pull a bird on a Saturday night. Which made the reality of my pulling abilities even more depressing.

The problem is that I was caught in a vicious cycle. I didn't believe I was attractive so went out trying to find a girlfriend to prove I was attractive. But because I thought I was hideous I had no confidence. Which meant no one would talk to me. Which made me feel even more ugly. Which knocked my confidence. Which meant I never found a girlfriend. Which proved my theory I wasn't attractive. But all I needed was to find a girlfriend! So I went out hoping to prove I was attractive. And so it continued.

The result was many sad and lonely nights in the pubs and clubs of Glasgow, standing awkwardly at the end of the bar trying to look taller and more confident than I actually felt. People with a poor self-image are often well-practised in pretending to be more confident than they actually are, the problem is that the façade that we build can quite quickly fall apart. Or in my case, make me fall over.

I've always had a real issue with my shoes. I like comfort you see, and that's not a matter of my sexuality (although brogues are quite common among the lady gays). I have very sensitive skin on my feet (I know, poor me) and an evening wearing high heels can leave me flayed raw. But I'd started hanging round with some people who weren't very good for my confidence. I know, what a surprise. One woman in particular took it upon herself to analyse me and provide me with her views on why I was so single and why, in her opinion, I would undoubtedly remain so.

You may have a friend like this. Someone who is happy to pick you apart and offer you support, which ends up feeding every paranoid thought you have about yourself. Of course, now I know she was actually a bit of a bitch who'd found a weaker member of the pack to feed upon. At the time I so lacked self-awareness and self-worth I was just delighted someone was speaking to me. She counselled me, head to toe, on my faults. Including the fact that I bite my nails.

Now, this woman was much older, well she was to me. She was probably in her early forties but to someone in her twenties she seemed as knowledgeable as Gandalf the

Grey. She had a proper job and a posh flat and I was slightly in awe of her. She had the confidence of an older dyke who felt that it was her role in life to tell me how I should behave to become a better lesbian. The conversation started badly, with me pretending to like Joni Mitchell to impress her. Unfortunately, I realised I was unable to name a single song Ms Mitchell had sung, leading to much ridicule. The evening then descended into a bottomless pit of awkwardness when she moved on to analysing the state of my love life. She started by slowly looking down at my hands, which at that point were mangled from nail biting, and proclaimed, 'You may as well give up. No one will ever want to go out with someone with disgusting hands like that.'

I didn't have the confidence to say what I should have, of course. To tell her that it was none of her business how I looked. That she was patronising and insulting. That she only went out with women three decades younger than her because anyone with an ounce of sense and maturity would run a mile from such a controlling bitch. But I didn't. I'm many things but I'm not rude.

After we'd finished with my horrific digits we moved on to other aspects of my appearance. She pinpointed my height as a particular problem. 'No one wants to go out with a shorter woman,' she exclaimed. 'It's embarrassing.' You may be screaming, 'Tell her to piss off Susan! She's a cow! She doesn't matter! Good things come in small packages!' And of course I should have dismissed her with a tiny wave, jumped down from my chair and walked off. I didn't. I asked her what I should do to make things better. She sighed, thought for a long time, and finally declared, 'Well, you could make more of an effort with your shoes. Maybe a pair of high heels would lift you up to a more acceptable height.'

And so I dumped my cherry red Doc Martens and I bought myself a pair of glamour shoes, high-heeled boots in fact. They worked for a while, if you think that someone standing at the end of a bar grimacing and sobbing gently is working. But I hated them. They weren't me, they weren't comfortable and I was acutely aware that even if someone did find me more attractive because I was taller I would eventually have to take the boots off. Then my true hobbit-like nature would be revealed. And I would be unmasked.

I don't want you to think that I didn't have some relationships during my teens and twenties. The Calman love machine managed to snare quite a few ladies in her web of desire. Well. About five ladies. And all of them cheated on me.

The truth is that a number of my relationships broke down because of my insecurities. Because I was too difficult for some to deal with. And I can understand, I suppose. Especially when you're younger, why would you want to spend your evenings working through your partner's issues when all you want is to be having fun? Of course, I would have done it, but it turns out not everyone is as marvellous as me.

I started to change my own view on relationships during the 'barren years', a sustained period of four years when I was resolutely single. For the first time ever, I gave up on finding love, and almost resigned myself to the life of a spinster. I imagined I'd end up swishing around town in a tweed cape and attending book groups or knitting circles of an evening for some sort of human contact. I became incredibly solitary in my outlook and it was not unknown for me to leave work on a Friday night, go home, shut the door, and not speak to a single soul until the Monday morning. I had Lara Croft and Tomb Raider for company. I pretended to my colleagues that I was totally busy with an exceptional social life, of course. I even used to order two dishes from my local takeaway so they didn't think I was on my own.

But I wasn't on my own, I had my cats. My wonderful furry friends to keep me company. You'll know by now that I adore cats, in fact I am a lover of all animals. And it may upset some of my feline fans to know that I was actually very much a dog woman before I was persuaded by a woman I was seeing to get a cat. It could be seen as yet another example of me not being able to stand up for myself, or as the greatest thing that's ever happened to me. My girlfriend at the time had a cat and before I knew it I had one too. I knew nothing about them and was, in truth, slightly terrified of them. They had razor sharp claws and an attitude problem. I think it took about a day for me to fall in love with my first cat. And after that they just kept coming. During the four years that I was single I was never lonely because I'd found, I believed, the truest and most wonderful relationship I'd ever have.

Of course, cats can be truly difficult. To quote the classic film *Terminator*:

'It can't be bargained with. It can't be reasoned with. It doesn't feel pity, or remorse, or fear. And it absolutely will not stop, ever, until you are dead.'

If you have a cat, you'll know that's no exaggeration. But I found it strangely comforting to have two furry assassins in my house. The solitude continued and I started to enjoy being on my own. I pottered along quite happily believing that it was better for all involved if I just didn't try to fit in with the social norm of partnership. I got used to the pitfalls of being single. For example, having pretend conversations with myself when the doorbell rang so that doorstoppers wouldn't think I lived on my own. And every Sunday I would go to McDonald's and buy a Happy Meal. Just because I could.

Until one day I had an epiphany, a moment when I had to admit that withdrawing from life wasn't the solution, and it happened in a most innocuous way. I was sitting in my pants on a Saturday night, playing the PlayStation as usual, when I happened to glance at the framed picture on top of the television. That's the place where one might display a photo of a partner or spouse for the entire world to see. What I had, in a cheap Ikea frame, was a picture of Gillian Anderson that I'd cut out of the *Radio Times*. In that sudden moment I realised that my most meaningful relationships were with a games console, two slightly disinterested cats and a woman from the television. This may ring true with you, it's like a moment when a giant light bulb goes off above your head and you think, *What the fuck has happened to me?* I decided at that moment

Susan Calman

that, to put it mildly, I needed to get out more. I admitted
to myself that I was lonely.

Many of my friends have used Internet dating to find love,
and I think for those who are shy or unsure or who just
don't feel like noisy pubs and clubs are for them, it's a
marvellous thing. It's crucial to be careful though. It's
easy to take advantage of us sensitive souls, and there are
those out there who can spot low self-esteem and take
advantage of it. But let me tell you my story and see if it
helps.

The year was 2003. I had a mobile phone but I don't
think that I had the credit history to be allowed to send
texts. There was no such thing as Internet dating, no way
of casually dismissing people by swiping their face left
or right. The landline was the king of romance. If you're
in your twenties you may be thinking that such times of
hardship could never have existed, but they did. Pay attention youngsters! This is how we used to do it. The first
step was to write an advert, and send it in the post for
it to be put in the back of a magazine or newspaper.
Hopefully another lonely lady would like what the advert
said, and would then phone up and leave a message on
an answerphone, which I, as Miss Lonelyheart, would
retrieve.

While I had the confidence to place the advert, one
thing hadn't changed. I still thought I was ugly and boring
and worthless. So I wrote an advert that was for the person
whom I thought the ladies of Glasgow would like to meet.
It went something like:

'Professional woman, late twenties, likes poetry, fine wine and exotic holidays, seeks similar for long walks and romance.'

The first four words of that advert were true. I know I was playing with fire but if I'd written an advert that truly reflected the way I felt would you have answered it?

'Professional woman, late twenties, likes staying in, avoiding looking in the mirror and eating Indian meals for two, seeks someone who will put up with a paranoid, depressed, short woman who has so far had minimal success with relationships for an unhealthy romance.'

The more astute among you will notice that there is one crucial piece of information missing from this whole affair. That's right. Never at any point in this process does either party see a photograph of their potential date. The only real information you had to go on to make a decision was the other person's voice, meaning that you had to make an instant judgement based on the short message that you heard on the phone. It might sound terrifying in this age of social media where we can track the bowel movements of a potential mate, but such anonymity had positives and negatives. On the plus side, for someone struck with a crippling lack of self-esteem, it means that you can't be dismissed instantly by someone who bases their opinions on looks alone. On the negative side, I didn't know what the person I was meeting looked like. What if they were hideous? Yes, that's right. People with low self-esteem can be just as judgemental as anyone else.

To sum up, I was going from a period of self-imposed glorious isolation to meeting people I hadn't met before (stressful social situation), who I didn't know what they looked like and they didn't know what I looked like (possible immediate rejection incoming), because I'd heard their voice (I make bad decisions all the time). It was a potential disaster waiting to happen. I was putting myself out there, not just with the single ladies of Glasgow, but with friends and colleagues who, even if they didn't admit it, equated personal ads with failure. And yes, you do need to tell someone you're doing this kind of dating, even if you don't want to. Tell someone where you're going and who you're going with, no matter how embarrassed you are.

Try and put yourself in my shoes next time you have a chance. Next time you phone the bank or an insurance company, listen to the person you're talking to. See if you can work out, just by the tone of their voice and their accent, whether you'd like them and whether you'd find them attractive or not. It is also an excellent way of livening up those annoying cold calls you get of an evening.

The first date I went on was a disaster. I met an earnest young lesbian who eyed me suspiciously when I went to the bar for a second beer in half an hour. I'm not a heavy drinker but I don't react well to a suggestion that I'm an alcoholic. She also had the outline of her swimming goggles around her eyes that gave her the appearance of a judge-mental owl. I didn't want to see her again but was still surprisingly upset when she didn't call me. Needy? Moi?

The next date I went on ended badly after a profound political disagreement. The one after that was with a police officer who told me that she was only doing it to make her current girlfriend jealous, which was a real confidence boost. Especially when she brought that girlfriend along on the date. I was fairly dejected but things got even worse after the next message I listened to:

'Hello, my name is Brenda. I'm twenty-four. Just got out of prison. Currently unemployed. But it means I have a lot more time to spend loving you.'

I admire someone who can spin a negative to a positive, but I really didn't think we would hit it off. And so I consoled myself with the fact that at least I'd made an effort and, anyway, no one would ever understand me the way that my cats and Gillian Anderson did. But then, quite unexpectedly, fate stepped in.

My advert was meant to run for a month, but for some reason it was printed for a week beyond the time I'd paid for. I ignored it until the last day, when I realised that my voicemail was still active. I'd had a few pints, got home and dialled. There was a message waiting for me from a strange woman who said she was leaving a second message after deleting the first one by accident after having too much wine. I was tipsy enough myself to find the idea that someone couldn't leave a simple message rather endearing and phoned her back. Fourteen years later it was the best drunk decision I've ever made.

*

After many years of trying to make it work with anyone who showed any interest in me, I struck it lucky with my wife because, not only is she terribly sweet when she's drunk, but I wasn't willing to settle. I needed her to know what I was like and to see if she could cope with it and help me through periods where I was quite depressed. And she can, although it's not been easy. We have been through some quite frankly horrific times together when I've been really low and probably quite frightening, but talking to her and telling her what I need means that we have a fairly good system in place to cope when the Crab of Hate has a particularly firm grip.

For example, when I start to lose perspective, which happens on a fairly regular basis, she lets me have a rant and then she presents me with the empirical evidence. It's almost a negotiation that she has to have with my head.

Me: Everyone hates me.

Wife: No they don't. I can name twenty people off the top of my head that don't hate you.

Me: I'm ugly.

Wife: I don't think you are, but more than that, if you look in the mirror you will see that you aren't. You have terrible self-image but you are not ugly.

Me: I'm a failure.

Wife: Let's sit down and go through what you've done and what you're doing and you'll see that you're not.

I know it doesn't sound like fun for her, and the flip side is that I try very hard not to let myself get to a crisis point. I also promise to listen to her when she gives me advice on ways in which we can be better and I can be better.

I'm also very lucky to have exceptional friends. Online as well as in real life. I've talked about the negatives that social media can bring, but it can be an incredible support as well. My job means that I don't see my real life friends that often, but when I'm home we go to the pub every Friday night and just shoot the breeze. They're used to my moaning, they know when I'm in a bad way, I don't need to explain myself, and they just cheer me up.

The network of friends and family that you have around you is crucial to your mental health. If you're reading this and feel alone, I understand that. As you now know, I've had times when I wouldn't speak to another living soul from Friday evening until Monday morning. I've joined clubs and societies to make friends, some of them were excellent, some of them less so. But the world is full of people just like you, who want to make friends and find people who they can open up to and laugh with. They are out there. They are. Keep a copy of this book on you at all times and then when you see someone else with one you can start a conversation.

CHAPTER 16

NEGATIVITY IS MY SUPERPOWER: A POSITIVE VIEW

ONE of the key things that I try to do is think positively about my depression. I tell myself that it's important, if at all possible, to make the best out of what can be a very bad lot. You might think that as a theory it's a) stupid, b) unachievable and/or c) easy for me to say. But it's a matter of trying to find any tiny, almost imperceptible, joy in the darkest hour. I've come to accept that I'm stuck with this head and these feelings, but what I can try to do is celebrate who I am and how I feel. To at least make sure some jaunty music or fireworks accompany the Crab of Hate.

It would be easy to believe from the contents of this book that I'm sad all the time, perhaps that I'm incapable of feeling joy. But that's definitely not the case. I can be happy, in fact I'm definitely happy a lot of the time. Improbable as it may sound, some things even make me delirious with joy. And one of the keys to coping with my depression is finding out the little things in life that make me feel at ease and taking the time to do them. I love a good cup of tea. Nice and strong, not a lot of milk, served in my favourite mug. I like the feeling when a train arrives on time. I adore it when one of my cats decides I'm good enough to use as a bed.

I haven't always been able to see the good in my situation, and I only really started learning to do this when I met my wife, when I started trying to change my ways and see things from my partner's point of view. My wife is one of the most placid human beings you could ever meet, almost always cheerful, kind and lovely in every way. It was because of her that I was jolted into the realisation that, if I was going to be like this for the rest of my life, I needed to make an effort to enjoy it. It was only when I pushed her to the very edge of her tolerance that I realised things couldn't carry on the way they were.

It was August 2010 and, as I've already explained, I was midway through the worst year that I had experienced at the Fringe. I didn't enjoy the show, the audience didn't enjoy the show, the numbers weren't spectacular and all in all I was miserable. The Crab of Hate was in fine voice with the paranoia, anxiety and general malaise following me round. My wife used to come through from Glasgow on a Friday night to join me for the weekend, and on this particular evening she met me after my show in the Cowgate area of Edinburgh. I was, of course, absolutely beside myself with misery. 'No one likes me, everything is awful, and I hate myself.' I think I spent half an hour or so whining at full volume about how terrible things were for *me*, how *I* was so hard done by, how no one understood how life was for poor, little *me*. It was at this point that my wife lost it.

She said what I suspect many people have wanted to say to me for many years. She stopped in the middle of street, looked me straight in the eye and shouted, really shouted:

'Fuck you. Do you think that the world revolves around you? Do you think that I haven't spent the week hating some of the things in my job? Do you think that all anyone ever does is sit and think about you all the time? They don't. When was the last time you asked me how I was, asked me if I was OK? You are selfish and you enjoy wallowing in your own depression. I love you but sometimes you're very difficult to love.'

It was shocking, not simply because my wife had never lost her temper before, but also because she was right. And no one had ever confronted me about it before.

My previous relationships had always faltered because I'm so set in my ways and hate doing anything that I don't want to do. My mother always says that my major fault is that I can't hide what I'm feeling, that my face always gives away what I'm thinking. And she's right. In previous relationships I'd sulk and moan and eventually partners got fed up with my moodiness. When I met my wife I fell in love with her the moment I met her because she seemed to me to have the kindest face I'd ever seen. I knew she was a good 'un and I was determined not to muck it up. So I started making an effort to enjoy what she enjoyed, to not throw a tantrum when I didn't get my way. It was tough, but this process of trying to see the positive in everything really helped.

For example, we have incredibly different tastes in films. I like action films, horror films, anything where I'm not likely to think about my own head. My wife likes animated films and movies about romance and timeless love. I cannot watch them. Because, as you will know from a previous chapter, I cry. A lot. I've never recovered from when she made me watch *Up*. The first ten minutes destroyed me. But I know she loves them so I try to think positively. I try to kick my mind into gear and think of something, anything, that is of use. After watching *Up* I took comfort from the fact that I'd never need to watch it again. I was forced to watch *Mamma Mia!* and decided that when I grow up I'd like to be Meryl Streep. Everything has something good going for it if you really look hard enough.

Here's another example, I often have problems sleeping, particularly during times when I'm feeling low. Insomnia has been a constant in my life from a very young age. Most of my childhood was spent lying in my bunk bed, wrapped in my Strawberry Shortcake duvet cover, staring longingly at my George Michael poster. On the good side, being an insomniac in 2016 is far more palatable than it was thirty years ago. Last night I listened to a few podcasts to keep me company in the wee small hours. In the days before technology, all I could do was sit and wait for dawn to come, occasionally flicking through teletext for company.

Don't think that I've simply accepted my fate. Name a remedy and I've tried it. Revolting tasting teas, a notepad by my bed to write down my worries. One book suggested the best thing to do was get out of bed and do some cleaning. So I did. And had to spend three weeks apologising to my flatmates for hoovering at 2 a.m. I'm so desperate for help that I've gone right outside the box to try to find a cure. A couple of years ago I went to Iceland and consulted an Elf Queen to try to get relief from my insomnia. She gave me a special stone to hold in my hand at night that would surround me with protective spirits who would sooth me to sleep. It didn't work. It's not particularly soothing to wake yourself up by smashing yourself in the face with any kind of rock. But I did get to hang out with an Elf Queen so it's not all bad.

Friends have suggested that I go to the doctor and get sleeping pills, but that won't help. The sad reality is that pills won't stop the main reason I can't sleep: namely, my restless and ridiculous mind.

Last night's thought process went something like this:

1. What's that song about being a bitch and lover and a child and a mother?

2. Was it Alanis Morissette? I loved *Jagged Little Pill*.

3. I should listen to *Jagged Little Pill*.

4. *Jagged Little Pill* makes me think of my first girlfriend.

5. My first girlfriend left me for someone taller.

6. Will my wife leave me for someone taller?

7. Where would I live if we split up?

8. I should probably learn how to change light bulbs in case I'm single.

9. I'd need a big ladder.

10. We used to play ladders in the Brownies.

11. Why wasn't I made a Sixer in the Brownies?

12. I wonder if Gillian Anderson was in the Brownies?

13. I've still got my Brownie uniform, should I wear it if I meet Gillian Anderson?

14. I fancy Gillian Anderson.

15. I fancy a biscuit. I fancy a mint Viscount.

16. How long it would take to read the whole Internet?

It helps to think positively about my insomnia. To think that I've been somehow chosen to stay awake and protect humanity, like a tiny brooding Batman, watching over the world as it sleeps. That might sound odd but at night, when I'm sitting at my desk knowing that everyone I love is asleep, I do take some pride that if a zombie apocalypse begins we will have a head start on all the losers getting their eight hours of kip.

Now when I'm at my most paranoid I prefer to think that I'm hypersensitive to people's opinions. That I care so much that I'm thinking about them even if they're not thinking about me. When I have periods where I can't get out of my bed for days, I like to think that I'm catching up on my sleep, all of the time that I miss when I have insomnia.

Let's face it, the world needs people like me. If everyone was an optimist nothing would get done right. Pointing out the potential flaws and obvious failures of projects means that everyone else ups their game. Depressed people are the catalyst to the success of the planet. Look at the banking crash. A bunch of people who thought they would make money forever. If I'd been there I'd have made it clear that it was a failure waiting to happen. Sometimes it's important to be hyper-worried, anxious and ever prepared for what might happen. I can't tell you how many times I've been proven correct when I've been worried about something. I am the voice of reason in a world that doesn't think enough about everything.

My depression often takes the form of anxiety, which I keep in check by being in control. As much in control as I possibly can so I can keep the feelings at bay. Being a control freak isn't a bad thing, I've come to realise that I am in fact brilliant at organisation. No one else can plan and execute a day trip like me. I am a ninja of time-tables and laminated plans. I take comfort from the fact that, far from being excessive and annoying, my anxious nature makes me a superhero.

And while I am undoubtedly annoying at times, there is no question in my mind that the way that I am makes life easy for my wife. Although she would never, ever, admit it. Here is a (non-exhaustive) list of times when I have

Susan Calman

been proven correct. Yes, I have kept a list. I like to produce evidence when required of my superb achievements.

1. I always book taxis very far in advance, leaving more time than you might think would be required to reach my destination. It's the one thing in life that you can rely on in me. I'm always absolutely ready to go. Not everyone is like that. You need to leave room for humans and their foibles. So if I'm catching the 8.40 a.m. train from Glasgow Central I will book a cab at 7.45 a.m. The journey is ten minutes. But then I'm at the station and there's no panic. My wife is always telling me that I'm over anxious, that I should relax, that there's no need to be there that early. So when she was coming down to London to join me for a weekend I left her to it. She booked a cab for 8.10 a.m. It didn't arrive (of course it didn't) and I received a call from her at 8.20 a.m. as she sprinted for the bus. I was the bigger person though; I didn't shove it in her face that she was wrong. I waited until I wrote a book so everyone could find out.

2. I need to know what I'm eating and when I'm eating it. I am absolutely capable of planning a week or so ahead so I am certain I will have food at the times I want it. My wife prefers to be all spontaneous about things, despite my telling her that it would go horribly wrong and she should just accept that the Calman way is the right way. But she persisted until I, in a moment of kindness, let her be in charge. We were on our honeymoon and I'll admit, dear reader, that in a moment of weakness I allowed the romance to get the better of me. I agreed to allow her to take control and we left the hotel to find a restaurant 'on a whim'. The problem is that Venice is one of the busiest cities on the planet and eating on a whim is nigh on impossible. What is possible is wandering around for hours being turned away from restaurants because they're all fully booked by sensible people. After an hour of wandering, my blood sugar level became dangerously low, and in a panic we took a table in the first place with a spare table. Which was a fish restaurant. I do not care for fish. I hate fish, not personally of course, I'm sure they're nice people. I was tired, I was hungry, and I knew that if we'd only planned the excursion like I'd said, we would've been eating nice food. I sat down, looked at the menu, and I started crying. And I continued crying for the duration of the meal. Because of this clear mistake on her part she has, quite rightly, never been in charge of what I eat again.

3. She still sometimes, quite rightly, gets upset at the lack of spontaneity in our lives and tries to make me more relaxed. We went to Paris for the weekend a few years ago, at a time when she still believed that change was possible. As it's the city of romance I decided to throw caution to the wind and do something crazy, something that would impress her. I went on Twitter and asked for suggestions of cool things to do in Paris, you know things that might be a bit off the beaten track. Someone tweeted me and said, 'Why don't you go to the Paris sewers?' I know what you might be thinking, but remember I was trying to be relaxed and not stressed and all spontaneous. So I didn't look it up, I didn't research it, I just left it as a surprise for my wife. To be fair, in my mind I was expecting something spectacular. I envisaged beautiful tunnels, filled with candles, while a boat travelled sedately along and a man sang the *Phantom of the Opera* to us.

The day arrived and I announced to my wife that I had a surprise trip planned just like she wanted. We arrived at the sewers, and to say that it was underwhelming would be understating it. There was a small office and sign that said 'Sewers, €5'. It did seem quite cheap for a city that was notoriously expensive, but perhaps the boat rides cost extra? My wife was unconvinced, but I reminded her that it was what she wanted. We walked down a spiral staircase and it became clear, very quickly, that the Paris sewers are merely the sewers underneath the streets of Paris. The only concession they'd made to tourists was there was a mannequin dressed in a boiler suit with a stuffed rat at its feet.

This was what she had wanted though. Without my preparation and my research this was where we ended up, literally in the shit. We wandered round for a while; the sewers are like a maze, and it takes about an hour to get out of it. All the while wandering round pits of faeces. It got far worse when the smell really hit me. I have a very sensitive gag reflex and can be sick at the drop of a hat. I had to tie a cardigan round my face and sprint to the end of the sewage system before I vomited on myself. As we reached the fresh air my wife reluctantly agreed that my anxiety actually meant that life was more fun and she'd never ask me to be spontaneous again. I win.

I'm not suggesting that it's easy to think positively when your head is a cesspit of self-hatred, but try. Even if it's a tiny speck of hope, it will help. So you think people are talking about you? Good. That means you're important. No one appreciates the job you do? That's because you're so super brilliant that you can do the job better than twenty people. You're amazing. You feel alone? That just means you're ready to let some other people into your life.

This takes practice, believe me, and it's something that CBT therapy really helped with. Changing the way that my mind reacts to certain circumstances and events, trying to trick it into not falling down the hole again.

CHAPTER 17

SO, WHAT ARE YOU GOING TO <u>DO</u> ABOUT IT THEN?

I'VE told you many stories in this book, most of which have been an attempt to bring some levity to a difficult subject. But there is no question that there are times in my life, as there may have been in yours, when things have got too much, where I've thought that there's no way forward.

Writing down my experiences is my way of showing you that, no matter how bad you believe things are, they can get better. The fact that I am still here at all says this. I have been as low as a human being can possibly get. I've spent hours wondering if anyone would miss me if I just ended my life. I have the scars from years of self-harming. And I shudder when I think of those times.

But I am here. And I'm doing OK. Not all of the time, of course. I still have times when the Crab of Hate attaches itself to me and refuses to move. But I manage to dislodge it using the techniques and knowledge that I've garnered from years of walking around with an imaginary crustacean attached to me. I find that how I deal with the cloud that descends on me very much depends on the type of sadness that I'm experiencing, so here are some of my ways of gaining control and, as the wonderful Taylor Swift would sing, shaking it off.

The 'sense of impending doom' times

You might be one of those people who manages to float through life without a constant feeling of unease in the pit of your stomach about, well, everything. Sadly, I often wake up with a heavy knot of fear lying squarely in my gut for no apparent reason. My ulcer plays up and my cats don't enjoy the slamming of kitchen cupboards and my foul language. I find fault with everything in life and want to crawl back into bed rather than wait for the inevitable, unknown disaster to happen. Such episodes can be rather self-fulfilling and I have been known to spiral into a week of wanting to hide in my homemade bunker (it's really a fort made from pillows in the living room, but it still counts). As soon as I realise it's happening, there's only a short window available to try and heave myself back into the light. I know that I need to force myself to make a genuine effort to have fun, to relax, to enjoy myself, to give myself a break. Over the years I've developed a few coping strategies when I get into a particularly bad Tasmanian devil rage, short instant bursts of fun to shock myself back to reality. They include:

1. Doing something I wasn't allowed to do when I was

a child. I don't mean anything bad like cocaine or murder, I mean something your parents wouldn't let you do, because it was too expensive or they thought it was too lowbrow. I'll go and buy myself a pick-and-mix, or wander in the rain without a coat on. Sometimes I go ten-pin bowling. By myself. In the middle of the day, because it still feels so dangerous! When I was younger, we weren't allowed to attend the newly built bowling alleys of Glasgow for various reasons, mainly because of the rough gangs of boys that my mother was convinced hung around there. So now, when I need cheering up, I go bowling, always wearing a bowling shirt I bought when I visited Graceland in America. I'm awful at it, but it doesn't matter. Every time I miss the pins I shout, 'Rough boys be damned, Mother!' and it cheers me up. I'll go to see a film that no one else wants to see and get popcorn and a hot dog that I always scoff before the adverts. Simple things, easy things, but important things. Anything that gives you a thrill just thinking about them, they are shots of much-needed adrenaline and joy when lethargy strikes.

2. An excellent way of stopping the mental rot is to eat something ridiculous. Again, this is your own choice, but I like to eat a prawn cocktail. A proper seventies' prawn cocktail with iceberg lettuce served in a big glass. Sometimes with a melon boat to keep it company. I've been known to indulge at 9 and 10 a.m. And then for lunch. Another excellent option is to stick my face in a large bowl of whipped cream. These days you can buy it already prepared, with added sugar, in Marks and Spencer. A morning of that, eaten with my hands while sitting in my pants, is enough to make anyone happy. Apart from someone who sees me do it. Allow yourself those moments to forget what you should be eating and instead eat what you want to eat. I had a superfood salad yesterday that made me feel anything but super. However, a large bowl of Angel Delight has never failed to bring a smile to my face.

3. I have a few films that immediately cheer me up. The best that I've found is *Tootsie*, an exceptional comedy starring Dustin Hoffman. Add a blanket, cup of tea and a sofa, and anything else that makes you feel better. Try to find that film or television show; seek out what makes you feel calm and content. One that soothes your soul. Do not, under any circumstances, watch anything that will make you feel more sad or angry. For example, the afternoon I viewed *We Need to Talk About Kevin* was an unmitigated disaster. In the same way that our environment can trigger depression, there are things that can cheer us up. Find them and use them as often as required.

The 'I'm very angry at someone' times

Often depression can be triggered by a genuine feeling of anger or resentment about someone or something. It could be a frustration with work or a relationship, or money or college. Certainly with me there is a tendency to obsess over that one thing to the extent that a frightening intensity can blind rational thought. Such feelings can be difficult for others to understand and need to be dealt with carefully. Sometimes I'm just angry for no reason at all. I have the insight now to say to my wife that I'm in that kind of mood when she can literally do nothing right. She's developed a coping technique for it now, too: her tactic is just to agree with me no matter what I say until the moment passes. And it works. Even if I say something utterly stupid like 'Roger Moore was the best James Bond' she'll nod and smile, knowing that it's just easier that way. For both of us

Now, after years of making homemade voodoo dolls, I try to be proactive. Do something, anything, about what is making you upset. Often frustration can come from feelings of impotence, that it doesn't matter what we do, or what we think, nothing can be changed. While that might be the case, how will we know unless we try? Join a political party if you dislike the one in power, volunteer at a charity if you can help on a local level, use the power of social media for good instead of Facebook-stalking your exes. Do something, try to change something. If you have problems at work, talk to someone about what you could do to make things better. I have a friend who was constantly upset at the passive aggressive behaviour of one of her mates, who was making her feel awful about herself through comments on social media. We talked about it and I offered a solution. Stop being friends with her.

If you write a list of the things that make you angry

and you find that it's the same things that are always making you angry, is there a way to stop interacting with them? It may not always be possible, of course, but try to find some way of changing the dynamics, of putting yourself in a proactive position rather than a reactive one. Take control of your life, it's yours after all.

The 'everyone is out to get me' times

Ah! Paranoia! My old friend. This one is a toughie, because paranoia is not exactly a feeling that can be reasoned with. I usually think that a) an individual hates me, b) I've been deliberately passed over for work or a social event because no one likes me, c) people are bitching about me or d) everyone is laughing at me. This is where the technique of using empirical evidence can really help. Think, sensibly if possible, about what has happened. Talk to someone you trust and explain how you're feeling. Sometimes even saying things out loud can make us realise that the scenario we are worrying about is highly unlikely. Try not to give in to it. Try to keep your head. My wife often remarks that I have conversations with her in my mind that haven't actually happened, and she's right. Before I talk to her about something I've usually played through all possible permutations of what she'll say at least four or five times, sometimes I've even become incensed with rage at her reaction when she's done nothing wrong. Don't try to second-guess. Live in the reality of a situation.

I often find that doing something that needs me to

think about something completely different entirely soothing. I watch a lot of cooking shows and in particular enjoy one of the *Masterchef* franchises based in Australia. They often do a 'mystery box' challenge where the contestants have to make a delicious meal from the contents of, well, a mystery box. The randomness of the challenge and the time limit is perfect for the purposes of distraction and so I set my own challenges. One hour to make dinner from the second and fourth shelf of the fridge and the first thing that I pull out of the store cupboard. Admittedly, making a delicious tea from oatcakes, aubergine, celery and lemons isn't easy, but I give it a try, dammit!

The 'everything is awful' times

These are the bleakest, monochrome times. It's the start of *The Wizard of Oz* when Dorothy wakes up to a black and white world that seems to have the joy sucked out of it. In these times it's fairly easy to dismiss everything around as shit, awful, terrible, etc., etc. A consequence of this mist is a tendency to think about everything other than what is happening at that precise moment. About the future, or the past, but not about the place you're sitting in at that very moment. Nothing has changed more in my life over the past few decades than learning to live in the moment. Now, before you say it, I know. It's one of those things that people say, like 'Cheer up love'. But I truly believe that this has helped my sense of perspective and happiness more than anything else.

Where am I right now? Who am I with? What are they saying? I'm absolutely guilty of thinking ahead to the next thing that's happening, or moaning about what might occur, rather than sitting with a friend and enjoying the time I have with them. At 6 p.m. I put my phone in a drawer so I'm not tempted to look at it, so I can focus on what's happening right in front of my nose. I like to plan and control every aspect of my life, because where I'm going and what I'm doing is an aspect of my life that I can take charge of when my head is all over the place. The problem is that planning and worrying can become the focus of life. If you stop and look around, you might find that things aren't as bad as they might seem. That there are nice people and excellent things to enjoy. It can be difficult to take a deep breath and let go, but it helps. Removing ourselves from our lives because they're too difficult is a common diversionary tactic, but life is still there. The key is finding the bits that are amazing and holding on to them.

The 'I can't cope' times

Anxiety is a cruel mistress. It makes you panic about all the things that you have to do to the extent that you're paralysed with fear about all the things that you have to do, which means that you don't end up doing all of the things that you have to do, leading you to panic about all the things that you have to do, etc., etc., etc.

This kind of event happens to me less often now because I plan everything. Every single second of every single day. Apart from the occasional days where I've planned to not plan everything. To a certain extent I have to live my life this way. Unfortunately, the market for feminist comics in Glasgow is less buoyant than I'd like, and so I spend most of my time working in London. That means I spend a great deal of time on the west coast mainline to London. I don't mind. I've got to know most of the crew on Virgins trains by name, I always sit in a certain seat and we often have a cheery chat to pass some time. A quick calculation reveals that in the last year alone I've probably spent about 936 hours on a train to and from the capital. That's 39 days of the past 365. What that means is that I have to be particularly careful to make sure that I get where I'm meant to be at the right time. I try to remove any possible glitch from the system, which usually means removing everyone apart from me from the process. My calendar is a thing of wonder to behold, detailing everything that's happening in my life. I've talked earlier in this book about my love of lists and it's true. I have a small notebook that I carry with me at all times containing lists of things to do, people to contact, important chores to complete. It means that I don't get anxious because at the end of the day I can look at the list, see that it's completed and move on.

Get a system. Implement the system. Take control of the things that make you anxious (if at all possible).

The 'I can't go on' times

I've had them. I really, really have. I know that feeling and it's terrifying. When there genuinely doesn't seem like there's a reason to go on, that no one would ever miss me, that everyone would be happier without me. I'm not going to tell you not to do something silly, because when things are bad it doesn't seem silly. The answer to this one is simple. Stop. This is absolutely the time to talk to someone. A GP, the Samaritans, a friend, a colleague. Talk to someone. Get the help that you need. Don't feel embarrassed or stupid or needy. You can go on. I am living proof of the fact that it's entirely possible to claw back from these terrible times and be happy. Talk to someone, reach out. Don't sit in silence.

These are simple suggestions that work for me. You will undoubtedly find your own simple ways of trying to address periods of depression. Undoubtedly I'm far better at it now that I was when I was younger. I now have the presence of mind and the desire to stop myself falling into a pit of despair. I also have the support of a group of caring friends and family who know me and know what I need.

The 'I'm not worth bothering about' times

When I was younger I used to love traditional British sitcoms – a particularly curious example of our cultural heritage, some of which can still be seen repeated on our television channels to this very day. If you're from abroad, or are too young to remember these fine shows, let me just give a bit of background. For decades, millions of us watched big, colourful shows that avoided subtlety like it was kryptonite. *On the Buses, Love Thy Neighbour, George and Mildred, Terry and June* are but a few of the comedy classics that I remember fondly despite the casual racism and homophobia that I now realise pervaded many of the scripts.

I mention this fondness for kitsch as background, so that you have some context for my love of one particular sitcom that, in hindsight, might as well be called 'The Susan Calman story'. The show that's burned into my mind was a Ronnie Corbett vehicle called *Sorry*. Again, if you are unaware, the aforementioned, Corbett is a much loved comedy star in the UK, and was the short one in a double act called The Two Ronnies. I loved the show not because I was watching another tiny Scottish person on the television but because of the title. It turned out that even from my very young age it would be a word that would dominate my life.

Sorry.

I say sorry a lot, in fact I tried to keep track of how many times I apologise during an average day but couldn't keep up with my own mouth. I apologise to everything and everyone even when I have absolutely no reason to do so. So far today I've said sorry to the following things/people/ animals:

1. The cat for asking her to move from the sofa because she was lying on the remote control.

2. The fridge for closing the door with too much force.

3. A company who hadn't delivered a package I ordered.

4. The cat for not paying enough attention to her.

5. My wife for waking her up at the correct time with a lovely cup of coffee.

6. My agent for asking her a question.

7. The man who delivered my shopping because I'd ordered a lot of tins.

8. The toilet after I slammed the lid.

9. The cat for stepping over her when she was blocking the door.

10. Andrew Neil on *Daily Politics* because I missed something he said and I had to rewind the television.

It's a fairly common trait in those with low self-esteem to apologise even when there is nothing to apologise for, but the long-term effects of such prostration can be far more insidious and damaging. It's difficult to increase one's self-confidence when every sentence starts with 'I'm sorry to ask' or 'I'm sorry but can I just say'. It immediately suggests that whatever thought might be about to be expressed isn't really worth listening to. One might as well say: 'Don't bother paying attention to me, I'm not important!'

Part of the challenge that I face while trying to stay cheerful throughout my depression is to attempt to change the way that my brain functions, to alter learned behaviours that contribute to my condition. So I'm not going to apologise about the following advice, here are some of the ways in which I've tried to stop being Ronnie Corbett:

1. Sometimes I'll apologise and my wife will stop me and ask, 'Why? What have you done?' For example, she arrived home from work last night and I'd made dinner. It was a slightly strange dinner, one of those ones you make with the specific aim of using up everything in the fridge that's about to reach the sell-by date. She walked through the door and the first thing I said was, 'I'm sorry the dinner is probably awful.' Before she'd even tasted it, the very first thing I did was apologise for spending an hour making her dinner. She quite rightly pointed out, in a nice way, that I was an idiot.

I think, on a deeper level, I like to apologise right at the very beginning of a conversation so that I get it in first before I disappoint anyone. Which is precisely the problem, because by doing that I am negating what could be a brilliant idea (or dinner). So before you apologise, ask yourself the very simple question, *What do I have to be sorry about?*

2. Have you ever worked with someone who just says

what they think, with confidence, and if someone doesn't like it they just shrug it off and suggest something else? Imagine being that guy? Visualise walking into work or a social situation and, instead of immediately undercutting yourself, you say, 'Hey! I'm an intelligent person with a lot of ideas, listen to me!' It's not easy, and saying sorry becomes a habit that is hard to break, but it can be done. Make an effort to stop yourself before you speak and make sure that you only apologise when you do something that you need to apologise for.

3. Sometimes people who have depression are selfish, annoying bastards. If you are, then an apology is very much required. However, more often than not, I end up saying sorry for things that I can't really control. 'I'm sorry I'm feeling down' or 'I'm sorry that I've been crying.' It just adds to the general sadness of the whole situation, and my wife, who is legally obliged to stay with me now we are married, gets annoyed because she feels it's a slight on her. She hasn't asked me to apologise for the way that I am, nor does she want me to. It wastes valuable emotional energy to constantly feel bad about feeling bad.

It's symptomatic of a desperate lack of self-worth, but it's incredibly destructive to the perception that others can have of us. I want to be seen as a strong independent woman who kicks ass like Sarah Connor in *Terminator* or Lara Croft in *Tomb Raider*. Neither of these women ever apologised before leaping over a car bonnet and punching someone in the face. Living with depression is a jigsaw puzzle where all of the parts have to fit together in order to get better. Spending an hour a week with a therapist might help, but only if you analyse your life and start to make changes. Be honest with yourself, think of positive ways to alter the smallest details, like the language you use about yourself.

In order to try to change my behaviour, my wife suggested that I start to thank her, not just for being amazing (although she is) but as a way of retraining my mind from the negative to the positive. Once you start doing it it's tricky but really worth the effort and the difference is extraordinary:

'I'm sorry I feel so down' becomes 'Thank you for listening to me'.

'I'm sorry I ruined today by being grumpy' translates to 'Thanks for watching box sets with me when I didn't feel like going out'.

'I'm sorry for being paranoid' is more appropriately expressed as 'Thank you for reassuring me when I was wobbly'.

Not only is it an important change for the depressed among us but, according to my wife, she appreciates being thanked instead of the automatic response from me implying that she must in some way be annoyed with me. Eliminating the automatic response that I've been so used to has made a marked difference to our relationship and the way that I feel about my own mood.

Identifying any small trigger that can alter the course of

a depressive period and doing something about it is hugely important. If I'm about to slip into a down period, instead of just accepting it, I'll tell my wife and we will try to do something about it. Just yesterday I was feeling a familiar tweak of paranoia, the Crab of Hate was gently pinching me and making it clear that no matter how hard I tried I would never get to where I wanted to be. Instead of simply accepting this, my wife and I had a chat and I told her what I needed her to do. Essentially, I need the negative thoughts in my brain to be swamped by positive ones. I asked for twenty-four hours of compliments, the theory being that if I was bombarded by someone bolstering my confidence I might start to believe that I was worthwhile.

And it worked, it wasn't perfect of course, but it reduced the length of time that I felt down and also the force of the feelings. I appreciate that I'm lucky in that I have someone I've been with for fourteen years who is happy to spend the time that I need making me feel better, but having a mental health buddy of any kind is important. As with everything, it's up to us to be outspoken about what we need and to say it clearly but without apologising.

I'm not sorry that I feel the way that I do, but I thank my wife for understanding. I thank her for slowly persuading me that I am worth something, that I don't need to apologise for who I am. I start every day by looking in the mirror and saying to myself, *You are worth something, you are important, you're not a failure.* One day, one wonderful day, I'll wake up believing it.

Like everything in life, it's not easy to make changes, but the results are worth it. Start the day determined to alter destructive behaviours towards yourself or indeed others. Make every move a positive one. Do something about how you feel. Take action. Take control.

Change things.

Get better.

CHAPTER 18
SOME NEARLY FINAL THOUGHTS

I'VE talked a lot in the chapters of this tome about me. Reading a book is a one-way thing. Even if you're listening to the audiobook, technology as it currently stands doesn't allow you to interrupt and ask questions. You don't have the ability to pop into my house and challenge my thinking with your own opinions, which I'm glad of. Not because I don't want criticism, it's because I sometimes write in bed and I don't believe my wife would be pleased to come home and find strangers in our boudoir. And so my conclusions will lie here, etched in ink as testament to my own theories as to what helps make the Crab of Hate a tolerable companion.

You may agree with me, in which case you will perhaps feel reassured that you're not alone and things can get better. Which is good because it means that I've done my job. You may be so incensed with my cod psychology that you want to prove me wrong and show the world that there's another way of working through the clouds of depression that hangs over you. Good! That means I've done my job. Because the thing that is most dangerous is not talking about mental health at all. The secrecy and fear that surrounds the condition is the fault of many, including those of us who have it and are afraid to speak out. The perception of mental health won't change over-night. It won't be altered by a concerted effort by main-stream media, which sometimes seem to quite enjoy the narrative of madness as a story. And our overstretched NHS can only do as much as is possible with shrinking budgets and competing priorities.

In my view, this has to be a ground level revolution. One that starts with us, with people, with individuals. Asking genuine questions, actually listening, bringing some normality to the condition. Because the fact is, it's now more normal than ever to have depression (some would say that if you haven't at some point suffered maybe you're the weird one). This is something that we need to do without the help of governments or doctors, to make talking about how we feel the norm, not the exception.

I started to get better when I started talking about how I felt. And the only problem I have now is that I can't stop. I can't stop telling people how I feel. I can't stop trying to get other people to tell me how they feel. My wife, who has been blessed with an even temperament and very few emotional problems, lives in fear of me saying the words: 'But how does that make you feel?' I sit with the cats and try to get them to tell me how they feel. I ask telemarketers how they feel; even the postman avoids me now.

After years and years of trying every possible avenue

to sort out my Crab of Hate, I've found that my solution is extremely simple. By talking about my depression I've started to feel strangely positive about it. I feel quite fond of the fact that I have a less than cheery view on life. There are plenty of positive people in the world, and I cancel out most of them every time I open my mouth. The world needs people like me, the people who point out the flaws, the naysayers, and the dark philosophers.

Looking on the bright side, I've retained much of my teenage attitude for thirty years, which means I've technically never grown up. Also, having a downbeat view on life means I'm never disappointed. If you expect the worst of people and things, you're always pleasantly surprised. If I get home and I've not been burgled, I've won a small victory. If I buy a pair of shoes and they don't cut my feet to shreds, then I've succeeded. Optimism has always been uncomfortable for me to deal with.

My Crab of Hate is still there, except now I've bought it a hat. A top hat in fact, and it sits at a jaunty angle. And now I've got some ear muffs which block out the sound. And I know how far I've come. I'm standing on stage in front of complete strangers, telling them how I feel. I'll even draw you a picture if you like. It's a duck sitting next to a cat, but you'll get the drift.

It still doesn't feel quite right. But then I'm never going to. And that's all right. Just don't sit next to me on the bus. Unless you want to be there for a while.

It's very good to talk, to tell someone how you feel. Except if you hate this book. Then you definitely shouldn't. Why not have a salad to cheer you up? I hear that works a treat. Remember, if you don't agree with my thoughts, I don't mind. As I said before, feedback is always welcome using the hashtag #SusanIsAwesome.

I told you at the start of this book not to do what I told you to, but that was a bit of a fib. Because you should listen to me about one thing. And it's the most important thing I could ever say.

Go and talk to someone about how you feel.

And keep talking.

A SCENE FROM THE PRESENT DAY: AND IN THE END

AND so another day of glamour as a well-known Radio 4 comedian ends with a nice cup of tea and custard cream. I brush the crumbs from my shirt, haul myself from the sofa and wander to the bedroom followed by numerous cats and a wife in a weird conga line of Calmans. The lights go off and the snoring begins again. Luckily for me, my insomnia kicks in and I'm given the gift of a few extra hours to contemplate life, the universe and everything.

I know that I've lived through a lot and survived it all. Without question I've made things more difficult for me than they could have been, and others have been less than helpful than I would have liked. But I'm still here. This is who I am and this is what I have. Peace of mind is still my great aim, confidence sometimes wavers on my journey, but the strength of purpose I've developed is never lost.

I'm an odd woman with odd ways, but that makes life

interesting. More than that, I'm proud of who I am, whatever anyone might think of me. I'm a depressed, foul mouthed, angry, serious, intelligent, passionate, emotional, angry, sensitive, polite, feminist comedian. And I love every bit of me.

I am Calman. Hear me roar.

ACKNOWLEDGEMENTS

I wrote this book but it's been created through the kindness of a lot of people.

Lisa Highton and all at my publishers who, for some reason, wanted me to write this thing. You've been patient and wonderful and I thank you for everything.

My family who were legally obliged to take care of me until I was sixteen and then kept going out of love. My wonderful friends who put up with me. Vivienne Clore who is essentially in charge of everything I do and guards the gates of Calman Towers with a fierceness that is exceptional and beautiful. Fenner, Vernon-Smith and everyone at BBC Radio 4 who have provided a great deal of love and support over the past few years. Comedy types who I love and who inspire me like Sarah Millican, Katherine Ryan, Bridget Christie, Sandi Toksvig, Corry Shaw and Emma Kennedy. Writer types whom I adore, Muriel Gray, J.K. Rowling, Denise Mina and Val McDermid. My children/cats Idgie, Muppet,

Oscar, Daisy Fay, DCI Jane Tennison and Pickle, who keep me company all day while I write. Stevie, Lesley, Laura[2], and the wonderful Rhona Gemell, for beer and laughter.

And my wife, Lee, without whom I doubt I'd get out of bed in the morning. After reading this you might wonder why she stays with me. I wonder myself sometimes. Thanks, pudding.

USEFUL STUFF

If you need any further information on mental health issues or anything else contained in the book you might want to have a look at some of these websites.

www.mind.co.uk
www.time-to-change.org.uk
www.nhs.uk/conditions/stress-anxiety-depression/pages/
mental-health-helplines.aspx
www.samaritans.org
www.stonewall.org.uk

ABOUT THE
AUTHOR

Susan Calman used to be a corporate lawyer and in her time has worked on Death Row in America, at the United Nations in Geneva and been in charge of Vacuum Cleaners and Microwaves at an electrical superstore.

In 2006 she decided to give up her promising career in the Law to be a comedian. She reached the semi-finals of the BBC New Comedy Awards and 'So You Think You're Funny', was a finalist in the prestigious 'Funny Women' competition in 2006 and she hasn't stopped since.

In 2007 Susan was cast in 'Ugly Kid', a sketch show which was a sell-out at the Edinburgh Festival and, following critical acclaim, was commissioned as a pilot for Channel 4. The show was renamed 'Blowout' and the cast went on to be awarded a Scottish BAFTA that same year.

On Radio 4 Susan has appeared on *The News Quiz*, *The Unbelievable Truth*, *The Now Show*, *Dilemma*, *So Wrong it's Right* and presented *Woman's Hour*. She recently recorded her first sitcom for Radio 4 and her third solo series *Keep Calman and Carry On* was broadcast in 2016.

Sometimes Susan is allowed on television and has so far acted in *How Not to Live your Life*, Rab C Nesbitt, *Dead Boss*, and *Fresh Meat*. She's also appeared on *Have I Got News for You*, *QI* (which she won), *Don't Sit In The Front Row*, *Comedy Rocks*, *Show and Tell*, *The Matt Lucas Awards*, *Dara O'Briain's School of Hard Sums*, *8 Out of 10 Cats*, *Would I Lie To You*, and Comedy at the Fringe.

Susan continues to gig around the country and has always been a massive hit at the Edinburgh Fringe. She's recently finished her first UK tour and has started writing her next show 'The Calman before the Storm' which will debut at the Edinburgh Fringe in 2016.

Her first DVD 'Lady Like', which was recorded at the Citizens Theatre in Glasgow, is on sale now.

Susan lives in Glasgow and is lucky enough to be married with four cats called Oscar, Pickle, Daisy Fay Harper and DCI Jane Tennison. The cats are amazing.

susancalman.com
twitter.com/susancalman
facebook.com/Susan-Calman-44711520390

TWO ROADS

Stories . . . voices . . . places . . . lives

We hope you enjoyed *Cheer Up Love*.
If you'd like to know more about this book
or any other title on our list, please go to
www.tworoadsbooks.com

For news on forthcoming Two Roads titles,
please sign up for our newsletter.

enquiries@tworoadsbooks.com

TwoRoadsBooks